WITHDRAWN

C20th

ANTIQUES

THIS IS A CARLTON BOOK

Design and text copyright © Carlton Publishing Group 2003
Picture copyright © Martin Miller 2003

This edition published in 2003 by Carlton Books Ltd
A Division of the Carlton Publishing Group
20 Mortimer Street
London
W1T 3JW

A CIP catalogue for this book is available from the British Library.

ISBN 1 84222 927 3

Senior Art Editor: Diane Spender
Design: Brian Flynn
Production: Marianna Wolf

Martin Miller

Edited by Janice Anderson

C20th

ANTIQUES

Over 250 of the Best Modern Antiques

Contents

Introduction

As each century turns into a new one, the furnishings and decorative arts of the past 100 years automatically increase in value. Now that we have entered the 21st century, more importance is being placed on designs from the 20th century.

The way in which antiques are viewed and valued is constantly changing. The definition of an antique as "a work of art, piece of furniture or decorative item of more than a hundred years old" has become more flexible as technology has speeded up and, consequently, the products of that technology have developed the invisible patina of age at a faster rate. The distinction, for instance, between "antique", "collectable" and "second-hand" has become very fuzzy in recent years. There are, for example, guitars on the market that cost a few hundred pounds a few years ago, and are now retailing at over £50,000. You could hardly label these as "second-hand". Curiously in this disposable age – or perhaps because so much is disposable – modern artifacts are valued much more by collectors than their equivalents were by previous generations.

It is not just the monetary value that makes a modern antique, though. There are three other factors to be considered: quality, rarity, and personal preference. If you are dealing in antiques purely from a commercial viewpoint – not a stance to be encouraged – then good quality and rarity are your best bets for success. If, however, you are collecting for the right reasons, for the love of the subject and the items involved, then obviously you will need to depend on your own judgement, and if you find yourself with something not worth as much as you had hoped, then at least its presence won't offend you.

There are now a huge range of items that are considered collectable, from advertising, photographs, kitchenalia, rock and pop records, automobilia and luggage, to musical instruments; all have their place in today's market. The antiques business is fundamentally about knowledge, and even the best introduction to antiques cannot replace leg work as part of the learning process. Visit museums, specialist dealers, attend auctions and courses, and read books.

As with other periods, beware of fakes. Twentieth century furnishings carry marks and various other means of establishing authenticity. Remember that mass production made furnishings of this century more available, and items should be priced according to fair market value.

Arms & Uniforms

Warfare in the twentieth century was world-wide and took place on land and sea and in the air. An impressive amount of collectable arms and uniforms is the result.

The history and art of warfare has always fascinated collectors. The weapons and uniforms of twentieth-century war are of particular interest because ordinary men and women became more closely involved in the actions and consequences of war than ever before. Even if they or their relatives were not actively involved themselves, cinema and television brought it into their everyday lives in vivid detail, arousing a keen interest in possessing mementoes of the battles and other events of war and of the men and women who fought in them.

Interest in arms and uniforms today extends from the actual fighting equipment used to the often magnificent uniforms worn and ornate weapons carried on ceremonial and full-dress occasions.

For uniforms and arms to have lasting value, they must be in good condition and as complete as possible. This basic rule can be set aside if an item has a particular interest because of the name of its wearer or it the battle in which it was used is known: a beret worn by General Bernard Montgomery, victor of the Battle of El Alamein or U. S. General George Patton's famous ivory-handled revolvers would be splendid centrepieces of any collection of twentieth-century arms and uniforms.

Welsh
Guards
Bearskin

1980 / height 64cm / £585

The Welsh Guards are a regiment of the Guards Division of the British Army.
Their full dress uniforms, especially their bearskins, are a familiar part of
British pageantry. This NCO's bearskin carries the Welsh Guards' plumed
insignia and has a brass restraining strap. The headgear is current issue.

Kriegsmarine Colani Jacket

1940 / medium size / £315

The German Navy, particularly its submarines, or U-boats, played a significant part in World War II, causing great damage to Allied convoys in the North Sea, the Atlantic and the Mediterranean. This rare Kriegsmarine Colani Jacket was worn by a Haupt-Feldwebel – the equivalent of the Royal Navy's Coxwain rank – in the German Navy. The jacket is given added value because it has all its original buttons and a breast eagle decoration and shoulder boards signifying the rank of its wearer.

Dagger

World War I / length 70cm / £70

Daggers have been used by fighting men to thrust and stab in close combat since ancient times, often as their only weapon. This World War I German fighting knife, made by Ern, a weapons manufacturer, would have been just one of several weapons carried by its owner. It has a studded wooden handle and is complete with its leather and steel sheath.

Commando Knife

1944 / length 30cm / £85

Commandos were special military units set up by the Allies during World War II to carry out organized raids against Axis forces. They took their name from an armed force raised by the Boers in South Africa during the Boer War, which ended in 1902. This British Commando fine and deadly sharp fighting knife is made of steel and brass and has its original scabbard.

Life Guards Boots

1950s / height 43cm / £150

The British soldier's life is not all fighting, especially if he is in the Royal Regiment of Life Guards, which is part of the Household Cavalry. A Life Guards trooper has a splendid ceremonial uniform, descended from the great days of eighteenth-century warfare, to be worn on such occasions as the State Opening of Parliament and at royal weddings and funerals. Now fighting in tanks, the Life Guards trooper is still horse-mounted for ceremonial occasions, when he wears magnificent black leather boots such as these, which date from the 1950s.

World War II Flying Helmet

1944 / £185

Pilots of the Royal Air Force have a particularly romantic and heroic place in the British mind, particularly when "the Few" fighter pilots who won the Battle of Britain in 1940 are concerned. The pilot who wore this flying helmet was of a different order. His aircraft, probably a bomber rather than a fighter plane, flew at high altitudes and his helmet was designed to cope with these conditions. This helmet is an RAF "C" type flying helmet equipped with intrinsic radio earpieces, MK VIII goggles with a webbing strap and an H-type oxygen mask.

Automobilia

The twentieth century's greatest love affair was with the motor car and it continues today, demonstrated by the demand for all kinds of motoring memorabilia.

So large is the market for anything connected with motoring and cars from mascots, club badges and parts such as grills and steering wheels of famous marques to ephemera like car log books, garage signs and racing programmes, that anyone interested in automobilia, however modest their resources, should not find it difficult to amass a collection likely to increase in value over the years.

Most interest among automobilia collectors today is centred on car clubs, race tracks and the personalities of the car-making industry and of motor sports, especially grand prix drivers and rally drivers. Car clubs, both general clubs and clubs devoted to individual marques, flourished in Britain between the wars, a period when club membership badges and car mascots were at their most ornate and attractive. This was also the period when the Donington and Brooklands motor courses were at the height of their popularity. Ephemera and photographs related to them are just as popular as material connected with today's tracks, such as Silverstone and Monte Carlo.

Other good starting points for automobilia collectors are toy and scale models of cars, and the brochures for new cars, which are a type of memorabilia that tends to increase in value.

Rolls–Royce Mascot

Pre-1914 / height 17cm / £1,250

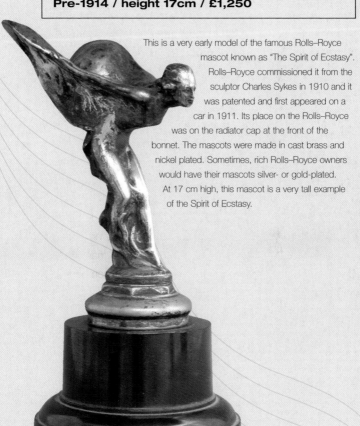

This is a very early model of the famous Rolls–Royce mascot known as "The Spirit of Ecstasy". Rolls–Royce commissioned it from the sculptor Charles Sykes in 1910 and it was patented and first appeared on a car in 1911. Its place on the Rolls–Royce was on the radiator cap at the front of the bonnet. The mascots were made in cast brass and nickel plated. Sometimes, rich Rolls–Royce owners would have their mascots silver- or gold-plated. At 17 cm high, this mascot is a very tall example of the Spirit of Ecstasy.

Mercedes Radiator Grill

c.1950 / width 65cm / £100

The perfect ornament for the home of a car fan, this Mercedes Benz radiator shell, with its shiny grill and star mascot, radiates style. It is made of chromium-plated pressed steel. The grill appeared on most Mercedes saloon cars from the 1950s until the early 1980s, although by that time its shape had become slightly lower and squatter.

Morgan Pedal Car

1980 / 122cm x 50cm / £950

The Morgan sports car has been very popular with British drivers since the mid-1930s. This neat scale model pedal car version of the Morgan 4/4 Roadster would have quickly turned the child it was given to into as big a fan as its father. The car has a fibre-glass body and chrome detailing. Its headlights and horn all work.

Bugatti Pedal Car

Late 1920s / 165cm x 56cm / £3,500

Ettore Bugatti's motor company, established at Molsheim in 1909, when the town was in Germany, became French when Alsace was returned to France in 1919. The company produced some notable Bugatti racing cars that were stars of the motor racing track between the two World Wars. This two-seater replica is a scale model of the Type 35 Grand Prix Sports Bugatti Eureka, made in France in the 1920s. It has very fine chrome and leather detailing.

Speed Award Badge

1920–1930 / height 16cm / £3,500

The Brooklands Automobile Racing Club was one of the most prestigious of the pre-World War II motoring clubs in Britain. It issued speed award badges like this one, based on the design of its members' badge, which showed cars banking round the Brookland's motor course, until it closed in 1939. This badge was awarded to drivers whose cars attained a timed lap speed of 130 miles per hour or more on the outer circuit. The red vitreous enamel label indicating the speed is rivetted beneath the wings, in the place where the "B.A.R.C." label would normally go. Since only about a dozen of these 130mph speed awards were made, they are both rare and valuable.

Brighton & Hove Motor Club Badge

_c._1920s / diameter 6cm / £200

Membership of a car club was something to be announced with pride in inter-war Britain, and there was no better place to announce such membership than on the radiator cap on your car's bonnet. This members' badge of the Brighton and Hove Motor Club was specially designed to be attached to the radiator cap and has since been converted to stand on a trophy base. More recent members' badges have been designed to be screwed to a car's bumper or other place, as cars no longer have exposed radiator caps. The badge is made of die-cast brass, which is chrome-plated, and the badge details are created in coloured vitreous enamel.

Ceramics

Pottery and porcelain design and manufacture in the twentieth century have been marked by excitingly innovative changes in decoration and shape, making the ceramics produced during the century one of the fastest-growing sections of the collecting market.

For much of the twentieth century, collectors of pottery and porcelain tended to view the ceramics made in their own age as less interesting than that of the eighteenth and nineteenth centuries. As the century drew to a close a marked change in attitude took place, as people came to realise just how extraordinarily vibrant and innovative ceramic production throughout the world since the beginning of the century had been.

It was very much a design-led revolution, with shape, colour and pattern radically changing the look and feel both of domestic tableware and of the vases, bowls and dishes that decorated homes. Materials changed, too, with earthenware and stoneware used in preference to porcelain. The clays and glazes that were once the preserve of potters also came to be much more widely used in ceramic ware of all kinds.

The Arts and Crafts Movement in late nineteenth-century England and the great movements in world art, from Art Nouveau and Art Deco, though Modernism and Post-modernism, were all very influential in the way in which twentieth-century ceramics were shaped and decorated. Many of the twentieth century's great artists, architects and designers, including Pablo Picasso, Kazimir Malevich, Walter Gropius, Frank Lloyd Wright, Aldo Rossi and many others, often working to commissions from internationally important manufacturers, brought many innovative changes to both the shape and decoration of pottery and porcelain.

This has made collecting twentieth-century ceramics as much about collecting art as about collecting the antiques of the future. Because so much of it was produced in great numbers, it is all the more important to be sure, if a piece is being bought with its likely future value in mind, that it is in as near perfect condition as possible. There should be no cracks or chips on the body of a piece, patches of glaze should not have flaked off, and there should be no repairs or obvious restoration work.

British Ceramics

The best pottery and porcelain produced in Britain, most of it in England, in the twentieth century is noteworthy for its stylish design and form.

The heart of English ceramic production in the twentieth century lay in Staffordshire, in a group of towns so closely connected to pottery manufacture they were once called "the Potteries". Long-established here were such famous manufacturers as Copeland Spode, Wedgwood and Doulton. But ceramic-making has never been confined to central England, and pottery and porcelain makers working in all parts of Britain in the twentieth century have ensured an enormously varied choice of ceramics of all kinds for collectors to choose from, whether for immediate use and enjoyment or for long-term investment.

Jug & Bowl

*c.*1900 / height 35cm / £185

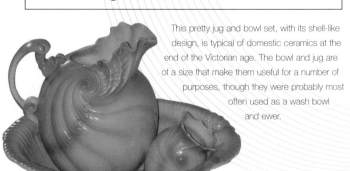

This pretty jug and bowl set, with its shell-like design, is typical of domestic ceramics at the end of the Victorian age. The bowl and jug are of a size that make them useful for a number of purposes, though they were probably most often used as a wash bowl and ewer.

Spode Cheese Dish

_c._1912 / height 6cm / £90

The Stoke-on-Trent, Staffordshire pottery company, Copeland Spode
began making their famous blue-and-white transfer ware
in the late eighteenth century. Spode still makes
it today, two of the most famous lines
being Spode Italian and the Blue Room
Collection. The landscape pattern on this
pretty cheese dish and cover harks back
to the style of Spode's earlier and very
popular Chinoiserie-patterned china, and
also looks forward to the countryside
scenes on today's Italian pattern.

Royal Worcester Cup & Saucer

1951 / height 7cm / £335

Fruit and flowers have long played a big part in the patterns on the porcelain of the Royal Worcester
manufactory, which was founded in Worcester in the mid-eighteenth century. The company's output
since then has been enormous, with very fine quality ceramics of all kinds being manufactured.
Royal Worcester's twentieth-century production continues to be large, much of it of very high quality.
This cup and saucer from a Royal Worcester tea service has gilding, a feature of much of its
production, on the rims of the saucer and cup and inside the cup and on its base and handle.

Royal Doulton Figure

1954 / height 14cm / £110

Figurines have long been an important part of the output of
the Royal Doulton manufactory, which was established by
the potters John Doulton and John Watts at a potworks in
Fulham, London in 1815. This figurine of a young woman
in sixteenth-century court dress, entitled Catherine
Clergon Sitzendore, was made when the Coronation
of Elizabeth II in 1953 had aroused interest in figures
with any sort of royal connection.

Royal Doulton Figure

1977 / height 29cm / £125

Royal Doulton gave the title "Harmony" to this elegant figurine of
a young woman standing posed in an evening dress, apparently
about to powder her nose. Dress and hairstyle are carefully
designed to show no particular fashion, and certainly bear
little resemblance to what young women were wearing
at the end of the 1970s.

Royal Doulton Figure

1968 / height 14 cm / £110

This figurine of a young girl in vaguely nineteenth-century dress is typical of much of Royal Doulton's figure output in the twentieth century: pretty rather than elegant or sophisticated and designed to appeal to a wide market. The company gave girl's names to many of these figures, in this case, "Clarissa".

Spode Figure

1910 / height 12cm / £268

Figurines did not play as large a part in the output of Spode as they did in that of other English manufactories. This finely detailed figure of a woman in eighteenth-century court dress includes on the dress's skirt a chinoiserie pattern familiar to users of Spode household porcelain.

Kaffe Fasset Vase

Late 20th century / height 36.25cm / £600

Kaffe Fasset became well-known in the late twentieth century for the richly coloured, luxuriantly massed flowers, fruits and foliage that featured in many of his designs for needlepoint, tapestries and rugs. This stoneware alabaster vase, made by Highland Stoneware of Scotland, features a typical Kaffe Fasset leaf and fruit design, which has been freehand painted on to it.

Poole Pottery Pot

1970 / height 45cm / £580

The area round Poole in Dorset has long been a centre for the manufacture of pottery using the rich clay deposits there. The Poole Pottery, founded in 1921, has made a wide range of richly coloured and splendidly designed ceramics, many of them in earthenware and using in-glaze techniques. This pot, by Carole Holdan, features large lime green and darker green scrolls.

Poole Pottery Cat

Exact date unknown / height 28.75cm / £27.50

The rich colour of this splendidly moulded cat is a red living glaze, a type of glaze pioneered by Poole Pottery. It has been used on many of the pottery's most striking ceramics, including vases, jugs and plates, for several decades.

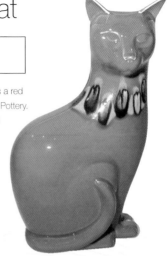

Highland Dish

1990s / 46.25 x 40cm / £189

Manufactured in the late 1990s, this octagonal stoneware dish is a fine example of the work of Highland Stoneware of Scotland. Its hand-painted design features lilies on a lustre ground. Lustre is a metallic coating that changes colour when it is fired.

McGowan Plate

Late 20th century / diameter 36.25cm / £250

With this delightfully designed plate, artist Lawrence McGowan looks back to popular china produced early in the century, which echoed the interest in nature and country life described in much of the poetry of the day. The plate's central pan depicts a tree alive with birds and berries, with the sun rising behind it. A haiku-style poem round the rim echoes the central subject.

Ocelot Vase

2000 / height 24cm / £411

This striking pottery vase painted by Catherine Mellor continues a long-standing tradition for making work with feline connections among English ceramic makers. The cat on this vase is an ocelot and the animal's fur pattern provides the rich blue background. The vase was made in other colour combinations by Dennis China Works.

Moorcroft Vase

1913–1917 / height 19cm / £575

William Moorcroft was a master potter who trained at the Wedgwood Institute at Burslem, in the heart of the Potteries. He founded his own company, W. Moorcroft Ltd, at Cobridge in 1913. Much of the work his factory produced used "powderfed" blue effects, raised outlined decorative effects and flambé glazes on fine wares. This splendid pomegranate vase is an early and typical example of his richly ornate work.

Butter Dish

_c._1940 / 12 x 18cm / £30

Even in wartime, British ceramic manufacturers were able to
continue turning out the simple yet charming household
ware that had been a staple of the industry for generations.
This cream ceramic butter dish with a lattice and apple
blossom design in relief is typical of the everyday domestic
china of the mid-twentieth century.

Troika Vase

_c.1965 / 36 x 17cm / £895_

Around the middle of the
century the Cornish firm of
Troika, St Ives, produced
some striking pottery that is
sought-after today. This vase
has a cream and turquoise
geometric design and a
rusticated finish.

Royal Doulton Vase

_c._1900 / height 28cm / £350

Lambeth Ware, named after the site of the company's first
pottery, was an attractive line from Doulton at the turn of
the century. This vase has a rim border of yellow and green
petals around darker coloured centres, and a lilac body.

Royal Worcester Bulb Vase

c.1930 / height 27cm / £850

This vase's name refers to its shape, not to its use, for it
is a flower vase, not a vase for growing bulbs in. Its
intense colouring – dark blue butterflies and birds on a
turquoise background – and oriental style is typical of
Royal Worcester porcelain and makes it much
sought-after by collectors.

Eduardo Paolozzi Plate

c.1950 / diameter 27cm / £150

The Scottish-born artist, Eduardo Paolozzi RA, has worked in many fields, including painting, sculpture and design. He designed this bone china plate for Wedgwood a few years after World War II had ended. Its bold red, black and gold geometric design is wonderfully expressive of the time when Britain was beginning to shake off the dreary after-effects of war and rationing.

Clarice Cliff Jam Pot

1934 / height 9cm / £750

This delightfully unusual jam pot is typical of the work of
Clarice Cliff, whose bright, jazzy designs have made her
one of the most sought-after English ceramic designers.
Most of her best-known work was done during the
inter-war period, when she was Art Director of the
ceramics firm, A. J. Wilkinson of Burslem,
Staffordshire. While there, she commissioned many
of the leading artists of the day to design a distinctive
range of earthenware shapes and decorations.

Susie Cooper Plate

1928 / length 26cm / £325

Susie Cooper was born in Burslem, in the heart of the Potteries in 1902 and was still
designing ceramics patterns in the 1980s. "Moon and Mountains," the abstract-style
pattern on this plate, was designed by Cooper when she was a leading designer with
the well-established pottery decorating firm, A. E. Gray and Co. They adapted the pattern
to many different shapes, including the ginger jar, a popular form in the Jazz Age.

Poole Ware Jug

1932 / height 13cm / £350

The colours – yellow, black and grey on a chalk-white
ground – set this small, attractively shaped Poole Ware jug
firmly in the 1930s. The abstract design and gently muted
colours are typical of many of the best
ceramics, furnishings and household
goods produced in Britain in
the 1930s.

European Ceramics

Pottery and porcelain production in Europe in the twentieth century was as wide-ranging and of as high a quality as it had been in previous centuries.

Much of the impetus for form and design change in European ceramics in the twentieth century came from opposite ends of the continent – Italy and Scandinavia. Also influential was the Germany manufacturer, Rosenthal, whose directors were happy to commission designs for their high-quality dinner services from artists from many countries. Throughout the century, architects, artists and designers in other fields turned their hands to ceramics, often with brilliant results.

Picasso Bowl

1952 / diameter 15cm / £755

Pablo Picasso discovered the pleasures of designing ceramics while living in the south of France. Working mainly with a pottery manufacturer in the town of Vallauris, he produced some of the most original and inventive pottery of the century. This wide-rimmed bowl, which has in the centre a stylised picture of a raven with stones at its feet, is hand-painted in a charcoal and grey wash.

Porcelain Busts

The German tradition for making fine, delicately decorated porcelain, much of it in manufactories in and around the city of Dresden, continued into the twentieth century. These porcelain busts of royal children are carefully made copies of the work of the great Meissen designer, J. J. Kaendler.

Italian Ceramic Vase

1950s / height 12cm / £150

In ceramics, as in many other areas of design and the applied arts, some of the most innovative work in Europe in the second half of the twentieth century was done in Italy. This three-sided, bottle-shaped vase with a pattern of abstract cartouches on a green ground was made by the ceramics maker, Cossa.

Asymmetric Vase

1950s / height 30cm / £40

This tall asymmetric vase, with its stylish green and white design on a black background, manages, despite its unusual shape, to retain the highly decorative elegance for which Italian ceramics were noted in the 1950s. The asymmetric look was popular throughout Europe at this time.

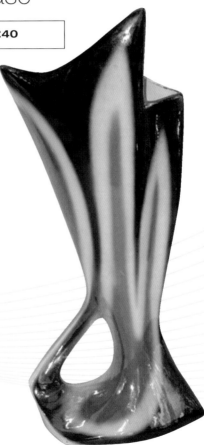

Ceramic Group

**20th century / height
39cm / £4,300**

The Italian tradition for making exquisitely
detailed figurines is well upheld by this fine
ceramic group made by Giovanni Grande
for the famous Lenci Factory. It depicts
Diana the Huntress after the hunt.

Tissue and Cotton Jars

c.1950 / height 23cm / £250

The prolific Italian designer Piero
Fornasetti was strongly influenced by the
surrealism that also influenced the style
of Italian cinema in the 1950s. It shows
here, albeit somewhat muted, in the
design incorporating mermaids and
scallop shells on these toiletry jars. Gilt
banding around the edges of the lids
adds elegance to the design.

Italian Ribbed Vase

1950 / height 33cm / £65

The incised ribbed pattern on this bottle-shaped, long-necked vase, made in Italy, was not uncommon in earthenware pottery of this period. A matt black finish adds to the elegant appearance of the vase.

Bosche Frères Vase

1920 / height 26cm / £280

Bosche Frères is a long-established firm of French ceramics makers. This vase, of oval form with a splayed lip, is a fine example of its post-World War I production. The geometric design is coloured with orange, black and cochineal glaze on a white ground.

World Ceramics

Europe's centuries-long love affair with pottery from many parts of the world was boosted by the importing of a wide range of goods in the twentieth century.

While the highest-quality porcelain from China and Japan fetches high prices, in acknowledgment of the time-consuming skill that must go into the production of cloisonné and enamel work, other more simply made and decorated objects from the world's pottery manufacturers, including a good range of houseware, still offer attractive bargains for collectors.

Quenti Pot

Mid-20th century / 65 x 45cm / £1,800

This very large, impressively constructed pot has a diagrammatic decoration. It was made by the Quenti people of the Amazon region.

Satsuma Vase

1910 / height 21cm / £355

Satsuma ware, much of which was made for the export market, is highly prized among today's collectors of Japanese ceramics. Its large size makes this lavishly gilded baluster-form vase, illustrated with figures in a garden setting and decorated with floral patterns, very interesting to collectors. Buyers should beware, however: Japanese Satsuma ware has become so popular in recent years that the market has been flooded with cheap and poorly designed reproductions made in the Far East.

Ceramic Pots

c.1930 / 29 x 18cm / £155

Everyday functional pottery from many parts of the world fits in well in the modern kitchen with the terracotta pots and dishes produced by many Mediterranean countries. These three pots were made in the first half of the twentieth century in Borneo but copy styles in use for centuries.

Commemorative Ware

Commemoratives are made as a record in permanent form of events and people that have played an important part in the nation's life.

They became a good line for British ceramic manufacturers when the Restoration of Charles II gave the nation something big to celebrate. So action-packed was life in the twentieth century, with changes occurring at bewildering speed at every level of people's lives, that there was little diminution in a trade that was very lucrative in the eighteenth and nineteenth centuries. Strictly speaking, commemoratives should be contemporaneous with the event or life being celebrated. Thus, a plate commemorating the Miners' Strike in the 1980s is a true commemorative, but a plate marking the 400th anniversary of the victory over the Spanish Armada in 1588 is not.

Margaret Thatcher Mug

YOU TELL'EM JOHN!

1991 / height 9cm / £33

This caricature mug, hinting that Margaret Thatcher, while no longer Prime Minister, is still pulling government strings, is in a long line of politics-based, satirical commemorative ware. Much more flattering mugs of Mrs Thatcher were produced during her premiership, many of them for electoral purposes. Royal Crown Derby produced a bone china loving cup in a limited edition of 650 to commemorate her third term in office.

Miners' Strike Plate

1985 / diameter 27cm / £58

This bone china plate, commemorating the great miners' strike of 1984–5, has a sad resonance twenty years later, with the fight to save Britain's coalmines long lost. The plate was issued by the National Union of Mineworkers, whose leader at the time, Arthur Scargill, was seen as a hero by miners.

Prince Charles Mug

1981 / £5

Not all the commemoratives made to mark the engagement of the Prince of Wales to Lady Diana Spencer in 1981 flattered the prince. This mug, based on a drawing by the celebrated cartoonist Marc Boxer, makes use of the prince's large ear to form the handle of the mug.

War Effort Teapot

1939 / height 14cm / £140

The thought that war against Germany was coming again, so soon after the end of World War I, depressed many British people. This teapot was part of a major propaganda effort to get the British into a fighting mood. Made by Crown Ducal, the teapot was given in exchange for aluminium utensils, handed in by their owners as part of the war effort.

Toby Jug

1940 / height 17cm / £125

Toby jugs were first made in Britain in the eighteenth century, with the jug's spout made in the form of a tricorn hat. Winston Churchill, Prime Minister of Britain for most of World War II, was commemorated in innumerable Toby Jugs. This one has him wearing the uniform cap of First Sea Lord, and with the ubiquitous cigar – Churchill's favourite PR accessory – firmly in his mouth.

Musical Teapot

c.1953 / height 13cm / £240

Britain's Royal Family is the commemorative market's most lucrative subject. In the twentieth century there were six changes of sovereign, three jubilees and innumerable engagements, weddings, christenings, birthdays and deaths to commemorate. This magnificent gilded teapot, roughly in the shape of the Coronation Coach, was one of thousands of items of pottery and porcelain made to mark the Coronation of Elizabeth II. The teapot contains a music box which plays the national anthem.

Clocks, Watches & Scientific Instruments

The fine workmanship and mathematical precision in construction that are essential elements in good-quality timepieces and scientific instruments ensure their attraction for collectors.

This is a particularly interesting area for collectors because scientific advances and inventions in the twentieth century led to radical changes in the way in which clocks and watches in particular, but also scientific instruments, worked. The century's many exciting art movements also had an effect on the look of clocks, watches and all kinds of scientific instruments.

Because timekeeping and measuring passing time, whether by calendar, clock, or noting the phases of the moon, has been important to civilised man since ancient times, the household clock has always been considered a particularly personal item. For many years it was one of the few items that was specifically mentioned in wills, along with the master bed and the home itself. Today, this close personal feeling for clocks is reflected in the considerable interest felt by antique collectors in them. The watch, which is actually worn on the person, usually on the wrist, but also in a pocket, has also seen a marked increase in collectors' interest over recent years.

Clocks, watches and scientific and marine instruments need to be handled with greater care than most other antiques, in order to prevent damage to their delicate internal mechanisms: it really is a matter of looking but not touching, and of going to an expert for even a simple cleaning. Many of them are housed in cases that could corrode or rust if not cared for, so where they are sited in the home also needs to be carefully considered.

Clocks

Electricity, in cell and battery form, and quartz technology brought radical changes to the way clocks worked and the way they looked in the twentieth century.

The clock-making industry was relatively slow to catch up with happenings in science and technology and it was not until the 1920s that electric clocks were accurate enough to become popular. With the design of the first quartz clock in 1928, clock-making really took off in new directions.

While many innovative clock designs were produced in the twentieth century, clocks with the appearance of old-fashioned bracket and carriage clocks, but with modern mechanisms, remain popular.

Desk Compendium

c.1902 / 15 x 16.5 x 6cm / £2,300

English-made clock movements were recognized as being among the best in the world. It is not surprising, then, that this high quality French desk compendium should have an English eight-day movement with its original silvered English lever platform escapement inside its gilt bronze and green enamel case. The compendium, which was a gift to a young man on his coming-of-age, 29 December 1902, was sold with its original leather travelling case.

Lyre Clock

c.1900 / height 49cm / £6,600

This attractive lyre-shaped clock, the lyre strings forming the moving pendulum, was made in France. The floral enamel dial which has arabic rather than the more usual Roman numerals, is surrounded by paste brilliants. The porcelain case, coloured in a deep blue called "Bleu de Roi", has gilded mounts and a gilded Medusa head in a sunray tops the clock. Inside the case is an eight-day movement that strikes the hours on a bell.

Hallmarked Clock

1904 / 20 x 10 x 5cm / £850

This small red leather and silver-fronted mantel clock, with its stylish Art Nouveau shape, would have looked very smart and up-to-date sitting on an Edwardian mantelpiece. The case has a "Birmingham 1904" silver hallmark and the white enamel dial, surrounded by a green enamel ring, has roman black numerals and black spade hands. Inside is an eight-day movement on a platform escapement.

Miniature Oak Clock

c.1900 / 35 x 10 x 7.5cm / £650

Longcase clocks, often called grandfather clocks, were first made in England in the seventeenth century. They soon became essential items in everyone's entrance halls – unless, of course, the house was small and the ceilings low. The early twentieth century saw numbers of miniature longcase clocks being produced for small houses. This English oak-cased miniature longcase clock has an eight-day French escapement movement, cylinder escapement and white enamel dial with black roman numerals and spade hands.

Mappin & Webb Clock

c.1911 / 37 x 23cm / £2,500

Bracket clocks – portable clocks with a coiled spring instead of weights and a short pendulum – are generally the most highly prized timepieces among clock and watch collectors. This elegant early twentieth-century English eight-day, double fusee bracket clock was sold by Mappin and Webb, the long-established firm of jewellers and silver-smiths. Its finely figured mahogany case has an olivewood inlaid panel and boxwood stringing.

Chagrin Mantel Clock

1920 / height 14cm / £2,750

This English-made mantel clock has a case covered in chagrin (or "shagreen") leather. Its white face and white ivory stringing and feet proclaim its period, white and ivory being fashionable in 1920s' design.

Watches

The story of watches in the twentieth century is very much the story of the wristwatch.

The first wristwatch was made by a Swiss watchmaker in the 1860s and by the early twentieth century the form had ousted the pocket watch as the personal timepiece that most people preferred to wear.

Lady's Wristwatch

c.1960 / diameter 1.5cm / £645

The house of Jaeger-LeCoultre has been making clocks and watches by hand at Le Sentier in Switzerland since the early nineteenth century. This quietly elegant lady's wristwatch has an 18ct gold case and leather strap. Its square face is an uncommon shape for a lady's watch.

Lady's Dress Watch

c.1930s / 1.5 x 1cm / £1,100

Platinum and diamonds join together in a glittering partnership on this delicately-designed lady's dress watch. The English case protects a movement made in Switzerland. The watch's "bootlace" strap, very typical of the period, is made of silk.

Cartier Watch

1968 / diameter 2cm / £2,250

The name Cartier is as synonymous with outstanding quality in watchmaking as it is in jewellery. The firm has been making watches since 1888, so this watch, made in the classic Cartier Tank design, marks eighty years of quality watchmaking. The watch has an 18ct gold case and a sapphire winding button. Its square face incorporates a white dial and roman numerals.

Rolex Oyster Perpetual

c.1952 / £35,000

The Rolex watch company is pure twentieth century, having been founded in 1905. By the 1920s it was conducting tests on watertight watch cases and patented the Rolex Oyster in 1925. In 1927 Mercedes Glietze swam the English Channel wearing a Rolex Oyster watch. Rolex was granted a patent for its Perpetual mechanism in 1931. Oystertight watch case and perpetual mechanism come together in this 18ct gold wristwatch with moon-phase calendar.

Rolex Silver Pocket Watch

c.1920 / diameter 4cm / £700

Pocket watches date back to the late seventeenth century, so it is not surprising that many men preferred them to wrist-watches, which were considered more suitable for women, in the early years of the twentieth century. For them, Rolex designed this silver pocket watch with a circular blue enamel insert to the outer casing of the watch. The figures on the watch face are arabic and the watch has a seconds dial.

Fob Watch

1910 / diameter 5cm / £223

A fob was a small pocket in or just below the waistband of men's breeches and, later, trousers, designed to hold a seal or watch, or other small item. In Edwardian times many men still wore fob watches and this is a classic example of such a watch. Made by Vetex Revue, the watch has a gold case and a white face with a subsidiary seconds dial.

Jaeger-LeCoultre Watch

c.1960 / diameter 4cm / £1,500

Not all high-quality watches are made with 18ct gold or platinum cases. This Jaeger-LeCoultre Memovox wristwatch has a stainless steel case with silver digits on a silver face. The Memovox was the first automatic wristwatch to have an alarm function.

Benson Watch

1940s / diameter 1.7cm / £250

This mid-price lady's wristwatch dates from the World War II period. Sold by J. W. Benson of London, the watch's 9ct gold case has fancy lugs for holding the watch strap. The white dial has easy-to-read arabic numerals.

Scientific Instruments

Collecting scientific instruments is in its infancy, as people are still waking up to the fascination of these often magnificent objects.

While still not as big as other areas of twentieth-century collecting, the interest in scientific instruments is growing and prices are rising accordingly for both scientific and marine instruments. For Britons, marine items, including chronometers, sextants, compasses and star globes, have a particular fascination, hinting at the romance of sail and the excitement of round-the-world yacht races.

Even so, since the usual rule-of-thumb – the older the instrument the higher the price – still applies, collectors interested in instruments made in the twentieth century should be able to make a fine collection for a relatively modest outlay.

A particular point that would-be collectors should be aware of is that with scientific instruments it is important that the original lacquer on the piece is intact so that the patina on it is preserved. If the lacquer has been removed, an expert should be asked to re-lacquer the item.

Corrosion is often a problem with marine brass and copperware. For a marine instrument to have any real value, it must be free of severe corrosion. Buyers should remember, too, that corrosion is not of itself a useful guide to age since items used at sea can corrode quickly.

Brass Microscope

c.1910 / height 34cm / £650

This pre World War I monocular brass microscope on a four-footed
stand has lenses giving the user two magnifications. It was made by
W. Watson and Sons, of High Holborn, London.

Anemometer

1950s / 8 x 9cm / £349

Anemometers, or wind gauges, are used in coal mines, flues,
ventilators and similar sites to measure the lighter currents of
air in them. This vertical and horizontal
anemometer is made of brass and
enamel and has a solid leather
case and accessories.

Armillary Sphere

Late 20th century / 93 x 59cm / £2,750

An armillary sphere is an astronomical instrument. Its rings, all circles of a single sphere, are so arranged that they show the relative positions of the principal circles of the celestial sphere – that is, the heavens above and around the earth. This large armillary sphere is made of polished and lacquered brass and has a wooden stand.

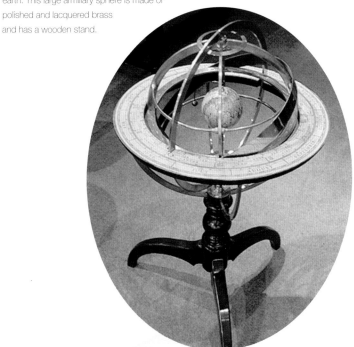

Brass Telescope

1910 / length 102cm / £2,900

This elegant brass telescope sits on a tripod foot. Made by Ladd of Chancery Lane, London, its sales value nearly a century later was enhanced by the fact that it was still packed in its original mahogany box.

"Faithful Freddie" Binnacle

Early 20th century / height 45cm / £1,250

Because it houses the ship's compass, a binnacle must be made of anti-magnetic material. This brass binnacle known as "Faithful Freddie", gained extra collectors' value from the fact that it had been used in a submarine and was later refitted to a little ship, for the evacuation of the British Expeditionary Force from Dunkirk in 1940.

Celestial Globe

_c._1950 / height 28cm / £1,280

A celestial globe is a model of the celestial sphere showing,
without distortion, the positions of the stars relative to each other.
This mid-twentieth century celestial
globe has brass fittings and is housed
in an oak box with a carrying handle.

Coins & Medals

Coins and, to a lesser extent, medals are so readily available that they offer beginners the chance to quickly build up interesting and potentially valuable collections.

Coins are among the most collected of all antiques. This is partly because their date and origin are usually easily read on them and partly because they require little space to store and display attractively. Medals, although there are fewer of them, are potentially of even greater interest to the collector because of their association with particular events in history and, often, with the people who were awarded them. While most medals have military connotations, others are of particular interest because they were awarded for service to people and society.

The twentieth century offers countless opportunities for collectors. Take coins: in Britain there were seven sovereigns whose heads appeared on the coins of the United Kingdom and the countries of the Commonwealth, and there was a major change to decimal currency. Wars waged throughout the century each brought large numbers of medals for those who took part in them, making medals the the most popular items among collectors of militaria.

Both coins and medals provide interesting ways to track the history of a nation and, by assessing their design and style, to judge the quality of that nation's art, culture and society.

Boer War Medal Group

1893–1902 / £1,800

The Boer War in South Africa was the last war of Victoria's long reign and the first of Edward VII's. It was a wholly British Empire affair and medals from it are plentiful and much sought after. This group of medals fetched a four-figure sum when sold because it was known that they had been awarded to a defender of Mafeking, Trooper A. H. Brady of the South Africa Light Horse. The medals are, from the left, a British South Africa Company medal for "Matabeleland 1893", a Queen's South Africa medal with three clasps, including "Defence of Mafeking", a King's South Africa medal with two clasps, and a South Africa Prison Services Long Service medal.

Gulf War Medal

1991 / £135

The Gulf War, fought to rid Kuwait of an Iraqi invasion force, was the last of the many twentieth-century wars that Britain's servicemen and women were engaged in. This Gulf War medal with clasp was awarded to Steward I. McMillan of the Royal Fleet Auxiliary.

RAF Flying Medal

1939–1945 / £950

This Royal Air Force's Distinguished Flying Medal (D. F. M.) was instituted
in 1918 for warrant and non-commissioned officers and men for acts of
gallantry when flying in active operations against the enemy and for acts
of courage or devotion to duty when flying. It has an appropriately
wing-shaped ribbon bar and this one, which was awarded during
World War II to Sgt. G. Jones, bears the head of George VI.

Third Reich Army Long Service Cross

1935-1945 / £225

A very fine specimen of Germany's gold Third Reich Army Long Service Cross, awarded for forty years' service. A gilt eagle standard and oak leaves are pinned on ribbon above the medal.

Purple Heart Award

1932–present / £24

The United States of America awards a Purple Heart medal for gallantry, to the wounded or to those killed in action in the service of the military forces of the nation. It bears the head of the U.S.'s first president, George Washington. This Purple Heart was awarded during the Vietnam War.

Edward VII Florin

1902 / £150

The pre-decimal currency florin was a coin worth two shillings (10 pence). This specially designed and enamelled – and scarce – coin was minted in the second year of Edward VII's reign. The coin is centred with Britannia, whose figure holding a trident has appeared on the reverse of English coins for centuries.

Burmese Rupee

1920 / £120

The rupee is a unit of currency in several Asian countries. This splendid Burmese rupee is centred with a peacock. Although it is of exceptionally high quality, it is an example of a coin quite commonly seen on the market and is therefore only of moderate value.

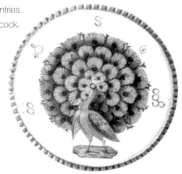

Collectors' Items

The term "collectors' items" is a convenient antiques-trade catch-all phrase describing the thousands of items that come dealers' way that do not fit easily into the major antiques categories, such as furniture, glass, ceramics and militaria.

A good many collector's items are covered by the old saying that what one throws away today, either because one no longer has any use for it or because it has been superseded by something that works better or is more fashionable is the collectable of tomorrow.

This being so, our grandparents should have kept their schooldays' pens and sports equipment, their 1930s Bakelite napkin rings, poker dice and tape measures, as well as all their smoking accessories and pre-war (both wars!) luggage. We should be keeping our first generation mobile phones, computers and computer game consoles and the games themselves, preferably in their original, pristine-clean boxes. All our long-playing records, tapes and CDs should still be to hand, along with their sleeves and boxes.

Of course, this is not possible: most people do not live in stately homes with large attics in which things may lie lost for generations. Which is a good thing because it means that there are always plenty of collectable items just waiting to be picked up from car boot sales, household dispersal sales, auction houses, market stalls and antique dealers.

Good advice for anyone thinking of building up a collection of unconsidered trifles is to begin with something in which they feel personally interested, whether everyday like biscuit or toffee tins or much more expensive, such as items of natural history taxidermy. This makes the search more interesting, amusing and, ultimately, worthwhile.

If building up a valuable collection, rather than a collection based on a personal interest in the subject, is the main aim of collecting, it is good to be able to recognize those things that were in some way groundbreaking, innovative or revolutionary, and not just momentarily fashionable, in their time.

Advertising & Packaging

As the consumer society grew, advertising and packaging became essential sales and marketing aids.

The "look" of the twentieth century owed much to advertising and packaging, whose requirements led to the creation of many new typefaces for lettering of all kinds and the invention of new packaging materials and ways of wrapping goods. The "corporate designer" appeared, giving companies a distinctive logo and other "looks" that set them apart from their competitors.

Dresden Figurine

1910 / height 17cm / £350

The woman and two children in this figure group made in classic Dresden porcelain style, are all carrying lavender, a subtle reminder that the flower has long been used as one of the classic scents and that its most reliable and acceptable purveyor is the English perfumer, Yardley. Established in the nineteenth century, Yardley still produce their English lavender products, especially soap, today.

Guinness Toucan

1955 / height 7cm / £250

The toucan bird and the slogan "My goodness – My Guinness" were for many years linchpins of the advertising and promotional campaign that helped sell great quantities of the stout produced by the Irish brewers, Guinness. This small ceramic promotional piece has the toucan by a glass of Guinness on a stand with the famous slogan printed round its edge.

Felix the Cat Toffee Tin

1930 / 16 x 16 x 10cm / £500

Felix the Cat was the first film cartoon cat, hitting the silent screen in 1914 and reaching the height of his fame in the 1920s. The competition from Mickey Mouse became too hot for him and he made his last film cartoon appearance in 1930, the year he was chosen to promote cream toffees by way of this attractive tin.

Gramophone Needle Tins

1910–1940 / 4cm square / £30–£100 each tin

The needles of wind-up gramophones had to be changed frequently, and even after each playing if the record in question was a particularly loved one. Needles were sold in tins like these, several tins being kept in the gramophone case. These tins come from a range of European makers, including Salon–Tanz Nadeln, National Band, Pathe and Sem-Aero-needles.

Rinso Box

1950 / height 14.5cm / £12

Soap powder in cardboard boxes was used in washing machines and for hand washing. The design on this Rinso packet, coloured the product's traditional green, shows wonderfully clean washing blowing in the breeze on a washing line. The theme was also used in advertising for the product.

Ceramic Coaster

c.1900 / diameter 16cm / £175

The Victorians turned advertising into a fine art, finding more and more surfaces on which to promote products. This white ceramic coaster, just the right size to take the foot of a beer glass, advertises Cannon Pale Ale, produced by the Cannon Brewery Co. Ltd, and bottled by Plowman and Co. Ltd, of London.

Collectables

"Collectables" are all those products of everyday life at home and outside that do not fit easily into the main antique-collecting categories.

Probably every room in the house, plus the garden shed and garage can yield a rich store of collectables for those with an eye to see them. On the bedroom dressing table you may find tortoiseshell combs, brushes and hair ornaments, powder compacts and pin boxes. The bathroom shelf might house razors, toothbrush holders and cottonwool and tissue jars and boxes. The study desk may contain letter openers, stamp boxes and visiting or business card cases and the sitting room could be home to magazine racks, draught excluders and record, tape and CD racks.

Outside the house could be more treasures, such as that meat safe or cheese cupboard hanging in a cool, shady place, or the old stone sink that was taken out to the garden to be planted-up with flowers, but never was. There might even be some fine old metal garden chairs and tables that need only a little tender, loving care to turn into very desirable items. And, of course, the garden shed could be full of very old gardening tools that are now very much sought-after.

As with collectors' items in general, the main thing to remember is that the ephemera of today could well be the antiques of tomorrow. Unless an item is broken beyond repair or is very badly worn, it may well be worthwhile to pack it away carefully in the attic for a few years.

Bakelite Pin Box

1930 / 8.5 x 3cm / £12

Bakelite, the world's first entirely chemically engineered plastic, may have been invented in the United States in the first decade of the century, but its cheapness and potential uses meant that by the 1920s it was being mass-produced throughout the world for use in a wide range of items originally made from many other materials, including wood, paper and cardboard, metals, glass and ceramics. This Art Deco-style pin box, in a typically rich and dark Bakelite colour, is English-made.

Bakelite Razor Box

1930 / 9 x 6cm / £35

According to the label attached to it, this dark brown Bakelite razor box is "a genuine TWO-TIX: opened and closed in two ticks." Inside this quickly-opened box is a Gillette safety razor. The presence of the box's original label, a promotional rather than an information-providing extra, adds to its value as a collector's item.

Royal Doulton Mug

_c._1940s–1950s / height 15cm / £65

Character jugs and mugs were a regular feature of Royal Doulton output in
the twentieth century. The name "Royal Doulton" is itself totally of the century.
Doulton & Co., who had factories in Lambeth, London and Burslem,
Staffordshire, in the nineteenth
century, became "royal" in
1901, under warrant from
Edward VII. This natura-
listically moulded mug is
in the shape of a Royal
Air Force pilot from
World War II.

Perpetual Calendar

Exact date unknown / £85

The measuring of the passing of time, whether by watch, clock, hourglass
or calendar, has provided collectors with a great range of interesting and
unusual items. This perpetual calendar, made in England in the early
twentieth century, has a handsome wood frame and turning knobs
for the three elements of the date shown on the front.

Handbags

The design of women's handbags in the twentieth century was notable for its variety and light-heartedness.

Women's handbags, especially those frivolous little ones usually called "evening bags", are wonderfully evocative of the period in which they were made and carried. When the emphasis is placed on elegant, stylish or amusing design, it does not matter if a bag's materials are expensive or cheap.

Brown Bakelite Bag

1950 / height 15cm / £395

Sturdy, hard to crack or chip and able to be produced in colours and patterns that could mimic tortoiseshell, silver, leather and other desirable handbag materials, Bakelite was widely used for women's bags in the 1950s. This brown Bakelite bag, made by Solar in America, has a foliate-design cover made from another "miracle" plastic called Lucite. This plastic had the ability to carry light round bends, and was used in surgeon's and dentist's tubing.

Black Beaded Bag

*c.*1920 / height 13cm / £295

Large enough to carry lipstick, powder compact and handkerchief, and, perhaps, a cigarette case, this elegant bag surely graced many a Jazz Age evening function. The black beaded bag has an elaborate gilded frame and clasp inset with diamante.

Red Plastic Bag

1930 / width 19cm / £395

Art Deco style makes way for the more technical style of the 1930s on this red plastic bag. The gold and black geometrical design on the front of the bag is carried on by the gilt chain handle, which is just long enough to allow the bag to be worn on the arm, thus freeing the wearer's hand.

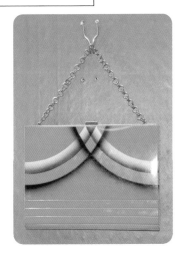

Petit Point Bag

c.1940 / width 21cm / £395

This traditional petit point evening bag has a tapestry-like picture that could have been made two centuries before. Worked in tiny silk stitches, the petit point decoration on the bag has figures on horseback outside a castle in a leafy landscape The bag has an opaline-beaded and enamel frame and catch. A gilt chain is attached to rings on the top of the frame.

Kitchenalia

As modern men and women spend less and less time cooking in the kitchen, so the interest in the minutiae of kitchen life continues to grow.

The demand for kitchenalia grew apace in the late twentieth century, fuelled in part by the great popularity of television cookery programmes and of the cookery books published in conjunction with them. Another reason for this growth in kitchenalia-buying is the fact that much kitchenware is still relatively inexpensive. It is easy to amass an interesting collection for a relatively modest outlay.

Potato Cutter

1940 / 26 x 12cm / £14

The "strongest and safest" implement World War II women could use to cut potatoes into chips was, according to the wording on its box, the new "Villa" french-fried potato cutter. The fact that the cutter was still in its original box, even if somewhat battered, added to its value.

Kitchen Scales

1940s / height 45cm / £45

This set of British-made "Popular" kitchen scales is accompanied by its original brass weights, which would have been set on the metal plate on the right of the scales, to counterweight the contents of the metal weighing dish, which is also original to the scales. The enamel paint on the scales is coloured in a shade of green typical of the 1940s.

Polka-dot Coffee Pot

1950s / height 18cm / £38

This pleasantly informal coffee pot, just the thing for morning coffee round the kitchen table, was made by Sandygate of Devon. The pattern of white polka dots on a blue ground suggests that the Devon pottery was hoping to produce kitchen pottery that would rival the famous blue and white striped Cornish kitchenware produced in the neighbouring county.

Bakelite Thermos

1930 / height 34cm / £11

The American Thermos Bottle Co. gave its name to a whole range of products. Just as many vacuum cleaners are called "Hoovers" and brightly mixed colours are referred to as "Technicolor", so most vacuum flasks are called "Thermoses". This elegant English-made jug-shaped thermos, clearly not intended for the picnic basket, is made of green Bakelite and has a metal handle.

Olympic Thermos

1950 / height 27cm / £65

This typically flask-shaped, handleless thermos, called the Vacwonder, is made of metal, and has a selection of sportsmen, including runners, cyclists, swimmers and shot-putters printed on the green-coloured background. The thermos flask was made to commemorate the Olympic Games.

Bread Board

_c._1940 / diameter 28cm / £28

Satisfyingly old-fashioned in looks and concept, this bread board is just the sort of thing that collectors like to have for everyday use in their traditional-style kitchens. It is made of wood and has a foliate design surrounding a central flower on the rim. It is clearly marked "Bread" to prevent its being mis-used for cutting meat and vegetables.

Bread Knife

1940 / length 31cm / £30

Just the right age and design to accompany the bread board above, this bread knife has a turned wooden handle with the inscription "BREAD" and a well-cared-for blade.

Salt Cellar

1930 / height 24cm / £55

The word "sel" on the front indicates that this hanging storage
jar for salt was probably produced in France. Made of enamel
with a wooden lid, it has a blue and white check pattern that
would help make it an attractive addition to a kitchen that
already contains the blue-and-white patterned china that has
been popular in English kitchens since the eighteenth century.

Luggage

Old luggage, which suggests travel to far-off, romantic places, or use in out-of-the-ordinary or far-from-everyday circumstances, is a popular collectable.

Most luggage, especially suitcases, hat boxes and travelling bags, made early in the twentieth century was leather, and was, therefore, quite heavy. In the days before maximum baggage allowances, this was not a major consideration for travellers which means that a great deal of it survives in excellent condition.

In recent years there has been a steady rise in demand, and therefore price, for luggage, especially leather hat boxes, picnic hampers and items made by Louis Vuitton.

Picnic Case for Two

*c.*1910 / width 28cm / £550

This leather picnic case, made in England, vividly recalls the Edwardian world of summer picnics, croquet on the lawn and boating parties that was swept away by World War I. The case is fully fitted with custom-made accoutrements, including a thermos flask and boxes for food.

Goyard Hat Case

1920 / 25 x 49cm / £1,500

No well-dressed lady went out without a hat in the 1920s and hats not being worn needed a case to carry them without damage. The body of this Goyard hat case is made of canvas with a painted chevron pattern on it. The trim is tan leather, held in place with small brass nails, and the case has a leather handle and brass fittings.

Sports Case

1930 / length 73cm / £800

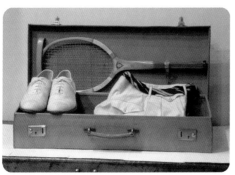

This tan leather cricket case with brass fittings and leather handle has been given leather straps in the lid to hold a tennis racket rather than a cricket bat. It was made by Finnegans of Bond Street, London.

Pens

**Fountain pens make fine gifts, and they are addictive
– buy one superb pen and the collector is hooked.**

These two facts explain why the pen is the mainstay of the writing
equipment market and is more keenly sought-after by collectors
than writing slopes or inkwells. Condition, strong colours and original
fittings are all of paramount importance in pens.

Parker Pen

1942 / length 12.5cm/ £380

Parker, Waterman and Sheaffer were
American companies which dominated
the pen market in the twentieth century
and their pens are highly sought-after
today. This Parker Victory fountain pen has
a case of black and green laminated plastic. Plastics were first used for
pen cases in the 1920s. Before this, pens were made of hardened
rubber, a much more expensive material.

Waterman Fountain Pen

c.1920 / length 14cm / £900

This Waterman 0552 fountain pen is gold-plated with a basketweave pattern.
Lewis E. Waterman's first major contribution to the design of the fountain pen
was the invention of an improved ink feed design that involved fine grooves
under the pen nib. It was used in his pens from the first years of the century.

Sewing Items

Most collectable sewing items come from early in the century when more durable materials were used.

Especially popular among collectors are such items as thimbles, measuring tapes and pin cushions. Thimbles should be closely inspected before buying because so many reproduction ones are made today by mail order companies specializing in "antiques of the future".

Porcelain Thimble

*c.*1900 / height 2cm / £210

This pretty porcelain thimble has a robin and roses painted on it Gold banding marks the top and the bottom rim.

Mouse Tape Measure

1900 / length 7cm / £175

The measuring tape is hidden inside the mouse, with the mouse's tail being used to wind the tape back inside. The mouse is made of silver and has pink glass eyes. Silver was a popular material for good-quality sewing items early in the century and was used for needle cases, pin cushions, thimbles and other sewing-related objects.

Smokers' Accessories

The cigarette made smoking and its accessories popular and fashionable at all levels of society.

Among the most collectable smokers' accessories are cigarette cases, especially those of the Art Deco period. Hallmarked gold or silver cases can be very valuable. The quality of the craftsmanship that went into the piece and its style also have a bearing on its value. Also much sought-after are cases for vestas – short wood or wax matches – and for the standard wood-stemmed safety matches. Cigar smokers' accessories, which can command high prices if in good condition, include cigar boxes, humidors and cutters.

Enamelled Vesta Case

1912 / length 4cm / £395

The hallmark on the rim of this silver vesta case shows that it was made in Birmingham in the early years of George V's reign. The enamelled flags on the front of the case are those of the Royal Yacht Club, for whom the case was made.

Satinwood Humidor

c.1910 / 12.5 x 23cm / £495

This elegant rectangular humidor was produced in England. It is made in the close-grained hardwood: satinwood, so-called because of its wonderfully smooth texture, and has ivory banding round the lid and the sides.

Cigarette Case

c.1900 / length 9cm / £1,550

This distinctly risqué cigarette case may well have been carried in a gentleman's pocket for showing to fellow club members or drinking companions, but – unlike similarly decorated cigarette lighters made much later in the century – not to ladies. The cigarette case is silver and the black-stockinged lady reclining against a large fan is painted in enamel.

Sporting Items

Memorabilia and artefacts with a sporting connection have risen considerably in value in recent decades.

So valuable is just about anything that can be described as sporting memorabilia that it has become a good revenue earner for sporting clubs, especially those connected with football and rugby.

A love of sport and an interest in it, fuelled by world-scale events such as the Olympic Games and the World Cup which are watched by television audiences numbered in many millions, ensures that sales of sporting memorabilia will continue to increase. The lesson to be learned from all this: never throw away anything with a sporting connection, from your football boots, tennis rackets and roller blading knee pads, to magazines and match programmes.

Croquet Set

1930 / £495

You do not need a very large lawn to play croquet on and the shape of mallets and balls does not change, so a seventy-year-old set will do just as well as a new one. It would more than do, if it was as stylish as this one, which is a portable set on a mahogany stand with brass handle and feet. The set includes four mallets, four balls in the traditional colours of red, black, blue and yellow, and hoops.

Wicker Creel

*c.*1940 / width 26cm / £55

Wickerwork creels like this one were the standard thing for carrying the day's catch before fishermen turned to plastic boxes. This one, which is in very good condition, has an adjustable leather carrying strap with fasteners.

Football Trophy

1900 / height 45cm / £775

This handsome football trophy is in the form of an early leather football with lacing held aloft on a silver foliate tripod stand. The trophy is silver-plated.

Black Rugby Boots

1930 / length 29cm / £165

The black leather has been well polished and the laces are wonderfully white – all of which adds to the value of these pre-World War II rugby boots. Cracks or loss of patina in the leather and detached stitching would all have reduced the value of the boots.

Treen

Treen means "made from trees", and any small item made from wood qualifies for the name.

Many treen objects are carved and turned, and the most popular woods for this are apple or pear, although most other fruitwoods are also suitable. They are all softwoods with straight grains, which makes carving easier. Not surprisingly, treen made in the twentieth century is not plentiful, partly because wood was supplanted by other materials and partly because wooden objects tend to be thrown away when they have outlived their usefulness. Good patina is very important in wood carvings, while cracks greatly reduce the value of an item.

Napkin Rings

*c.*1900 / height 2cm / £18

These sycamore wood napkin rings are fine examples of Mauchline ware, printed wood-ware made in several towns in Ayrshire, Scotland, from the early nineteenth century. Mauchline, more famous today from its association with the poet Robert Burns, was one of the main production centres. The prints reproduced on these napkin rings are British scenes, but they could also have been scenes from Burns's poetry, which appeared on many items of Mauchline ware.

Amboyna and Maplewood Dish

*c.*1910 / diameter 32cm / £145

This handsome dish is fashioned from amboyna wood, a light-brown wood with a speckled grain, and maplewood, a North American hardwood. The dish was turned on a wheel to make the decorative rings on the top. The four balls on which the dish rests are made of maple.

Money Box

*c.*1900 / 10 x 7cm / £48

The wood in this money box with a castellated edge is sycamore, a light-coloured hardwood of the maple family. The picture printed on the front is a view of Eastbourne, a popular seaside resort. Treen souvenirs were best-sellers in Britain's many seaside resorts for the first decades of the twentieth century, until plastics swept aside all competition.

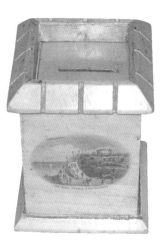

Taxidermy

Stuffed birds, fish and small animals were a feature of Victorian homes that was carried over to the Edwardian era.

The market for taxidermy almost disappeared in the first half of the twentieth century, such was the reaction against the over-decorated and over-filled houses in which our grandparents grew up. Since the 1960s there has been a steadily rising interest in the undeniably skillful work of the taxidermist, both as decorative items and as a record of the natural world. It has also become acceptable to have a favourite pet stuffed after death. An item of taxidermy will only be of good value if it is undamaged and is neither threadbare nor worn.

Mouse

Exact date unknown / height 13cm / £75

This little grey mouse has been sat in an alert pose on his hind legs, with forelegs raised, on a bright red apple. The apple is made of wax.

Eagle Owl

Exact date unknown / height 59cm / £260

This handsome eagle owl survives after death as a fine example of the taxidermist's art. The eagle owl is mounted on a tree stump set in an oval wood base.

Electrical & Radio Equipment

Inventors and designers grasped the opportunities offered by electricity early in the twentieth century. Electric light, the telephone, radio and television quickly transformed life in the home and the workplace.

The collector of the great electricity-based essentials of twentieth-century life has a wealth of material from which to build up a significant collection. However, because there is so much available, items have to be in good condition if they are to increase in value.

The range of lighting made in the twentieth century is enormous. Some of it – chandeliers and candelabra-shaped lights, for instance – looks back to the lighting of earlier centuries for inspiration and fits in very well in older, traditionally designed houses. Much more of it is designed with the modern house and its clean, functional lines and bright colours, in mind. While most electric lighting, however old, can function well, wiring and fittings should always be carefully inspected before use, as faulty connections can cause fires or electrocute anyone touching them.

The collector of old telephones is, sadly, not able to use his treasures in the same way as a light collector can because they do not fit into modern telephone operating systems. Because so many early telephones were made in black, collectors hoping to see the value of their buys increase should keep an eye out for coloured telephones. Coloured Bakelite was used for telephones in the late 1920s and coloured plastic became available in the 1930s. Even if a telephone is described as "novelty" by dealers, it is likely to increase in value in the future, particularly if it is still in its original box.

Radios should be bought in as near perfect condition as possible, and, although there may be bargains to be found at car boot sales, they are better bought from a reputable dealer who has restored and re-wired them well. Exceptions to this would be very rare radios, ones with the maker's name clearly on them, or very decorative examples. Pre-World War II radios with wooden fretwork cases, with a fabric lining behind which the loudspeaker sheltered, are attractive buys if the wood is in good condition.

Lighting

Many designers have been inspired by the possibilities of electric lighting to make interior light fixtures so fine that they are likely to become works of art in their own right.

Collectors buying light fixtures with an eye to their possible future value should inspect them very carefully for damage or missing parts. Many more ornate or cluster-style designs are individually made and replacing parts may not be easy. Lights made early in the century have considerable extra value if they have retained their original shades, which may be signed and therefore of value in their own right.

Pistillo Wall Lamp

1970 / diameter 60cm / £250

This Italian wall lamp – a starburst of silverized bulbs – is a Pistillo design by Studio Tetrarch of Italy.

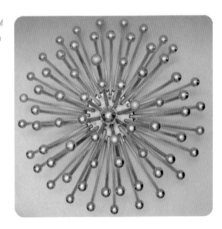

Brass Chandelier

1930s / 50 x 40cm / £375

This very pretty Italian brass chandelier is in a foliate design, with leaves "growing" out of the central "stem". The turquoise teardrop pendants are made of glass. The candle-shaped fittings hold flame-shaped lightbulbs.

Italian Tube Lamp

c.1970s / height 40cm / £1,200

The glassmakers of the island of Murano, in the Venetian lagoon, have been making wonderfully imaginative glassware for centuries. For this eye-catching light, a Murano glassmaker made tubes carrying a white abstract design within the glass and set them on a chrome cylindrical base.

British Spiral Lamp

Early 1990s / height 150cm / £980

British designer Tom Dixon made this lamp to create a great effect in a living room rather than a light to read by. From the light in the circular base rises a gold-coloured leaf spiral.

Italian Glass Lamp

_c._1950s / height 200cm / £750

Italian designer Guzzi seems to have turned to the cinema for
inspiration for this standard lamp. The heavy glass bowl-shaped
lamp rests on an ornate chrome stand.

Danish Lamp

1970 / height 120cm / £750

The epitome of Danish cool style, this tall and elegant lamp is
one of a series designed by Vernon Panton for the Danish
manufacturer, Louis Poulson. Materials used in the lamp are
metal, glass and plastic.

Radios

From the crystal set to the modern miniature transistor, radios display twentieth-century technology at its best

Key factors to keep in mind when looking for radios with possible antique potential are design and a Bakelite casing, as well as maker and age. The early radio maker Logie Baird and early – that is, pre World War II – combination radio and TV sets are much sought-after.

Croslen Radio

1951 / height 29cm

Bakelite, the first entirely synthetic plastic, transformed radio design, replacing wooden casing that made radios look like pieces of furniture with smooth, wonderfully coloured cases. Invented in New York in 1907, Bakelite was most widely used from the mid-twenties to the 1950s. This American radio, styled in the shape of a speedometer, has a Bakelite case.

Silver Tone Bullet 6110

*c.*1938 / height 17cm / £1,100

This radio has a very modern design for its period. Designed before World War II by Clarence Karstacht, it is a push-button radio with a very large rotating tuning scale.

Telephones

The telephone, the century's greatest tool for bringing people closer together, makes a great collector's item.

Telephones have great collecting potential, provided they are in good condition. Wood casings should not be split or their varnish lost and Bakelite should not have been exposed to destructive sunlight.

Blue Plastic Telephone

1960 / 14 x 14 24cm / £55

This telephone makes a splendid souvenir of the colourful "Swinging Sixties". It has a blue plastic case with a red dial on a cream base and a matching red flex and ringing-tone cut-off button.

Candlestick Telephone

*c.*1920 / 44 x 15cm / £395

The classic candlestick-shape telephone was the first successful compact desk telephone, replacing the earlier wall-mounted model. The shape was necessary to keep the transmitter upright. This example has a black Bakelite top and rim to the earpiece. The separate ring box is brass and wood.

Furniture & Furnishings

Furniture gives designers the chance to explore new designs and experiment with new materials on a small, relatively inexpensive scale. Thus, all the major cultural and design changes in twentieth-century life can be mapped by way of furniture and furnishings.

The dramatic visual and cultural changes of the twentieth century are mirrored in the furniture and furnishings of homes and the workplace.

Seating, the chair in particular but also stools and sofas, was produced in daring and radical form by designers and manufacturers in Europe, America and Japan. Chairs whose main materials were tubular metals, plastics and bent plywood, manufactured in bright colours, stood side by side with chairs made in traditional materials like wood, leather and cane or rush, but used in revolutionary styles and shapes. Tables, especially smaller ones, cupboards, chests of drawers and desks all bore signs of the century's design and material revolutions.

Although there should be a wealth of material ready to be snapped up by the enthusiastic collector of furniture, in fact, furniture with good value-increasing and antique potential is no more a glut on the market than any other kind of twentieth-century antique.

The main reason for this is to be found in the enormous changes in the way furniture was made during the century. Large-scale furniture-making following traditional methods was replaced by mass production and the standardization of parts that allowed furniture to be exported in knock-down or flat-pack form. Such furniture was not intended to last long enough to be the antiques of the future.

Furniture in the Arts and Crafts Movement and Art Deco styles, even if a specific designer or manufacturer is not known, is much in demand. Furniture made by the famous names of twentieth-century design, even if mass-produced, commands prices as high as other antique furniture, the market for which has grown enormously and spread across the world in recent years. If a piece carries a label or mark by the designer, design studio or retailer, so that identification of it can be precise, it is much more likely to prove a good investment.

Bookcases

Books were published and brought into the home in unprecedented numbers in the twentieth century.

The innovations in book publishing in the twentieth century – soft-covered books, paperback books, books printed in many colours on shiny paper that made them very heavy, "coffee table" books so large that the joke was they just needed legs to be tables in their own right – were not mirrored in any great changes in style of the shelves and bookcases in which books were stored.

Pair of Bookcases

> *c.*1900 / height 110cm / £5,500

Their restrained style and relatively small size help make these late Victorian-style open-fronted bookcases attractive additions to the furnishings of a modern house. They are made of mahogany, the hardwood most used in the production of furniture in England in the eigh-

teenth and nineteenth centuries. Inlaid decoration along the tops and stringing – fine inlaid lines round the edges – add to their elegant look.

Oak Bookcase

c.1910 / 190 x 80cm / £890

This tall, glass-fronted bookcase is made of oak, a hard-wood which tends to darken with age. The bookcase has an arched pediment and a curved base. There are two sets of doors, double glazed doors in front of the book-shelves and, below them, two panel doors.

Edwardian Revolving Bookcase

1901–1910 / 84 x 40cm / £1,450

The small proportions of this revolving bookcase, when compared with other examples of the style, make it an attractive item. It is made of mahogany and is on a stand with cabriole legs (legs that curve out at the foot and in at the top) and a shelf.

Bureaux

The radical change in the way people worked at their desks in the twentieth century meant that bureaux became desirable antiques early in the century.

The antique-dealer's definition of a bureau is a desk "with a fall front enclosing a fitted interior, with drawers below". The fall front, which becomes the bureau's work surface when let down, does not offer enough space or have sufficient strength to hold heavy typewriters or computers. But it will hold a laptop, there's plenty of room to write letters, cheques and greetings cards, and the compartments and drawers offer neat, out-of-sight storage for household paperwork and such essential items as pens, pencils, sticky tape, stamps, and paperclips.

Bureaux, like desks, are generally subjected to hard wear and so are often damaged, altered and repaired. If a bureaux is being bought with its future antique value in mind, it should be carefully checked. Handles should match and be original, the dovetailing on the drawers should marry up and escutcheons – the brass plate surrounding the edge of a keyhole – should be undamaged and original.

Pine Secretaire

Exact date unknown / height 80cm / £675

A secretaire is a type of bureau with a tall top cupboard and a false drawer front that is let down to reveal a writing surface and fitted interior. This miniature secretaire is made of painted pine. It has a broken pediment above the fall front, behind which is a full fitted interior. The secretaire sits on shaped bracket feet.

Walnut Bureau

c.1940 / 104 x 84cm / £1,895

Twentieth-century antique reproduction at its best, this elegant bureau is in the style
of the reign of George II – that is, the first half of the eighteenth century. It is made of walnut,
a hardwood used since the eighteenth century mostly in veneer form. The tassel attached
to the key is probably of more use in finding the key, should it fall out of the keyhole, than
letting down the front flap. The knobs on either side, below the flap, allow the flap rests
to be pulled out easily.

Art Nouveau Bureau

*c.*1905 / 120 x 90cm / £565

The Art Nouveau style is well to the fore in this Edwardian bureau, which has bookshelves as well as storage compartments. The organically designed metalwork on the single drawer is copper, a popular Art Nouveau metal, and the shaping of the woodwork is also typical. A ring-pull below the keyhole allows the front flap to be lowered easily.

Cabinets

**Free-standing cabinets for storing and displaying objects
continued to be made for the twentieth-century home,
often for items unknown in previous centuries.**

The free-standing cabinet has always been a more imposing place in
which to store and display valuable objects than the ordinary cupboard. In the twentieth century, cabinets were built to house things as
normal as the best china or porcelain figurine collections and as diverse
as cocktail-making equipment, radiogrammes and the records played on
them, and television sets.

Display Cabinet

**_c._1900 / 203 x 81cm /
£15,000 (the pair)**

This fine mahogany display cabinet is one of a pair.
It is made in the style of the eighteenth-century cabinet
maker, Chippendale and is in cylindrical form with a
pretty gallery cornice above the glazed doors. The
heavily carved and moulded base conceals two
double doors.

Camphor Wood Cabinet

*c.*1900 / 75 x 28cm / £1,680

Made in China in the late Ch'ing Dynasty (1644–1912) this black lacquer camphor wood cabinet is in three parts. It has gilded carvings and a couplet in Chinese characters that says "Man celebrates four seasons with festivals and self-attainment for all in quiet meditation".

Chinese Lacquer Cabinet

*c.*1900 / height 154cm / £980

The couplet in Chinese characters on the doors of this lacquer cabinet from eastern China is succinct: "Research in the art of craft. Writing on cookery skill". Lacquer, a common feature of Chinese cabinets, is a resinous substance which, when coloured, provides a background for chinoiserie and gilding.

Cocktail Cabinet

_c._1930 / 161 x 85cm / £995

Everything the Jazz Age cocktail-maker needed to mix the perfect cocktail
would have been hidden behind the doors of this elegant Art Deco cabinet.
It is made of figured mahogany and walnut in a circular design, not particularly
common in furniture but typical of Art Deco. It has a pull-out mixing surface.

Oak Cabinet

1895–1900 / 77 x 49cm / £420

The Arts and Crafts Movement at the end of the nineteenth century introduced a new simplicity into furniture design in sharp contrast to the over-elaboration and excessive size of much Victorian furniture. This Arts and Crafts oak cabinet has copper hinges and handle and a moulded and cross-banded door panel.

Carpets & Rugs

Carpets and rugs have been made by nomadic tribes in the vast region between the Caspian Sea and Western China since before the Greeks and Romans.

It is not surprising, then, that oriental carpets and rugs are a vast and sometimes bewildering subject for the would-be collector. Anyone thinking of investing in them would be well advised to read up on the subject in some of the many books that have been published on them.

For the less-intense collector, seeking a beautiful-looking rug in designs and patterns that have been woven for centuries, there are a few simple pointers to a good rug. For instance, counting the knots on the backside of a rug or carpet can give an indication of quality, because the closer the knots the better the quality.

Look out for any signs of fading colours (as distinct from the abrupt changes of shade over large areas of one colour that are inevitable with hand-dyed wools). Too much wear and tear on a carpet or rug will reduce its value, as will any obvious cutting or trimming of the fringe.

Qashqai Gabbeh Rug

Exact date unknown / 175 x 118cm / £1,050

This wool carpet of striking design was created without the use of dye, relying instead on the natural colours of the wool. It is a gabbeh rug, made by the Qashqai people of the Zagos mountains region of south-west Persia (Iran). "Gabbeh" in Persian means "fringe", though the word also means, when used for carpets, unclipped or shaggy-piled.

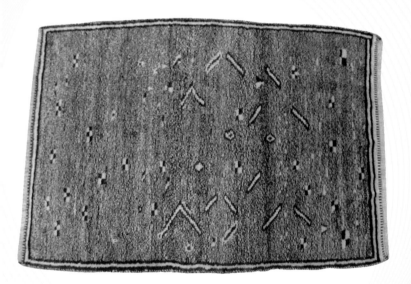

Striped Rug

_c.1920–1930_ / 122 x 120cm / £720

This simple, but effectively patterned antique gabbeh rug is typical of the distinctive weaving of the Lurs, a tribal group from the Luri region near the Zagos mountains of southern Iran.

Persian Rug

Early 20th century / 165 x 104cm / £760

This Qashqai gabbeh rug incorporates a strong central design within a geometric border on a red ground. The Qashqai are a tribal federation with annual migration routes, so their wide-ranging carpet designs, which are renowned for their vitality, influence other weavers in the region.

Western Anatolian Kilim Cushion

> **1920 / 35cm square / £45**

The cover on this cushion was originally a kilim, which are flat-woven rugs without a pile. The kilim was woven in the Western Anatolian region of Turkey. Some of the earliest Oriental rugs known are knotted pile rugs found in Anatolia in Turkey.

Shahsevan Cushion

> **1920 / 35cm square / £65**

Shahsevan, in northwest Iran, was the region in which the rug, made into the cover round this cushion, was woven. The rug was originally part of a cradle.

Karabagh Cushion

> **1920 / 35cm square / £50**

The cover round this cushion was originally a Karabagh kilim, woven in an unusual floral pattern.

Bownat Marriage Rug

*c.*1920 / 210 x 293cm / £1,650

This bownat marriage rug was produced by a small tribe in southern Iran. The rug shows courting birds and flowers within ornate geometric borders. The names of the couple about to be married, and the date of their marriage, are woven on the rug in Arabic. Such rugs are among the most beautiful examples of twentieth century tribal weaving from the south-western region of Iran.

Kilim-covered Chest

1920 / 50 x 90cm / £750

The flat weave and lack of pile of the kilim makes it ideal as a heavy-duty furniture covering, and it has been used on chairs and sofas as well as cushions. This beechwood chest is covered with a Western Anatolian kilim.

Kilim Stool

1930 / 30 x 40cm / £125

Brightly dyed and geometrically patterned, the Anatolian kilim from Turkey, with which this cabriole-legged stool has been upholstered, makes it a striking piece of furniture.

Sarouk Rug

*c.*1940 / 89 x 118cm / £1,100

Striking medallion compositions and rich colours are features of rugs from
Sarouk, a small village of just a thousand houses in western Persia (Iran). This
typical Herati design has a large medallion in the centre. The rug's background
colour is coral, with blue, pink and cream colours in the design.

Chairs

Chair design incorporated all the main themes of twentieth-century furniture design.

The chair, whether made in traditional or modern style, was used by most of the big names in furniture design to experiment with the new technologies, materials, and construction methods, as well as the theories of design, that were developed throughout the century.

The early Modernists, for instance, were more concerned with the theory of spatial harmony that also concerned architects than with the comfort of the chairs they were designing. Charles and Ray Eames, after World War II, used applied ergonomic theory to design chairs that supported the body properly. Then in the 1960s came chairs, such as the Sacco beanbag chair, that allowed each sitter to shape the chair to his or her own needs.

The fact that so many twentieth-century chairs were designed by people who became famous for their work means that the kind of chair that will become a twentieth-century antique is already an expensive buy. This makes it all the more important that the chair, whatever its style, should be in very good condition.

Egg Chair

1958 / 105 x 85cm / £4,000

The Danish architect and designer, Arne Jacobsen, produced several of the definitive chairs of the twentieth century. Fusing the furniture-making traditions of Denmark with Modernism, he produced such chairs as the light, stackable plywood Ant, and the impressive leather and metal Egg swivel chair. This version of the Egg in black leather is now a collector's item.

Cone Chair

1958 / height 84.5cm / £850

Verner Panton is a Danish furniture and textile designer who worked with Arne Jacobsen before setting up his own studio in Switzerland. His single-piece plastic stacking chair has become an icon of the 1960s. A little more conventional, in terms of Modernist design, was this slightly earlier Cone chair, on a metal base. Red wool upholstery covers the cushioned seat and backrest.

Finnish Leather Armchair

**1970 / height 80cm /
£1,500 the pair**

One of a pair, this moulded armchair
covered in tan leather, and with a metal
circular base, was designed by Wryo
Kukkapuro of Finland.

Swivel Office Chair

1970 / height 82cm / £600

An architect and a designer, Charles Eames was
one of the most innovative of American
furniture designers, working in partnership with his wife, Ray, from the mid-
1940s. This high-back office swivel and tilt
chair, with black wool upholstery and an aluminium stand on casters, is typical of their designs
intended for mass-production.

Sacco Beanbag

1968 / height 82.5cm / £800

Beanbags scattered about on an uncarpeted
floor, were a favourite resting place with 1960s'
hippies, students, and other laid-back people.
The Sacco beanbag chair was designed by the
Italian partnership of Pierro Gatti, Cesare Paolini
and Franco Teodoro. This red leather and vinyl
version is filled with polystyrene balls, enabling
the user to shape the chair to suit his or her
own body.

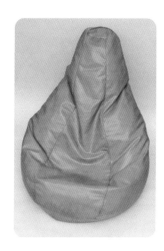

Seagull Chairs

c.1990s / height 75cm / £980 the pair

Arne Jacobsen's imagination took
flight when he designed these
Seagull chairs for Fritz Hansen, a
Danish furniture manufacturer.
Like Jacobsen's pioneering Ant
chair, these chairs have tubular
metal frames.

Rosewood Chair

c.1904 / 92.5 x 62.5 / £3,500

This Art Nouveau chair raised on turned legs with pad feet was designed in rosewood by Walter Cave for Liberty & Co, the London department store that did much to promote the Art Nouveau style in Britain. The chair is rare, hence its value.

Rocking Chair

c.1900 / height 87.5cm / £495

Not everything was in the Art Nouveau style at Liberty's. This simple rocking chair, with its rush seat and slat back on turned legs, owes much to the Arts and Crafts movement of the late nineteenth century. The chair was made for Liberty & Co.

Red Leather Chair

**_c._1960 / height 98cm /
£800 the pair**

The style of this chair, one of a pair, is typically Italian
of the 1960s: simple yet elegant lines and a touch of
the modern cinema. This chair is upholstered in red
leather, its partner in black leather. Both have teak
legs and back rest.

"Medea" Chair

**_c._1955 / height 82cm /
£450 the pair**

This is one of pair of moulded beechwood
chairs called "Medea" by their designer,
Vittoria Nobili. The beechwood is moulded in
one piece, with an oblong hole in the seat.
The straight legs are made of black metal.

Dieter Rams Armchairs

1962 / 69 x 86cm / £2,900 the pair

German industrial designer and architect Dieter Rams played a pivotal role in creating the look of the durable goods manufactured by the German manufacturer Braun, for whom he worked for many years, becoming the company's director in 1988. Rams designed these green leather chairs on a white fibreglass base for Vitsoe.

Art Nouveau Chair

c.1910 / 140 x 53cm / £825 the set

This leather-upholstered chair is one of a set of six Art Nouveau dining chairs. Made in oak, the set consisted of two carvers, of which this is one, and four single chairs, all with a slatted back splat and curved top rail above square tapered legs.

Arts and Crafts Chair

c.1905 / 88 x 44cm / £2,250 for three

This was one of three single chairs, probably all that remained of a larger set of dining chairs, made in the Arts and Crafts style. The chair has a moulded top rail and curved splat with fruitwood inlay and stands on straight, square legs.

Carl Jacobs Chair

c.1950 / 72 x 51cm / £485 for six

Teak became popular wood for furniture later in the twentieth century. Carl Jacobs used teak for the base of this chair, one of a set of six red moulded chairs. The chairs were made for the furniture manufacturer, Kandya Ltd.

Charles and Ray Eames Chair

c.1950 / height 84cm / £1,150

Husband and wife team of Charles and Ray Eames designed this bent birchwood chair for mass manufacture and marketing. It was made by the US manufacturer, Evans.

Red Stereophonic Chair

c.1960s / 129 x 86cm / £4,200

This chair was made to a special commission by the Lee Co. of California. It is a red moulded fibreglass egg chair on a circular metal base. It has grey and white wool-padded upholstery and leather-padded seat cover and back rest, with a fitted stereo. There is a matching ottoman.

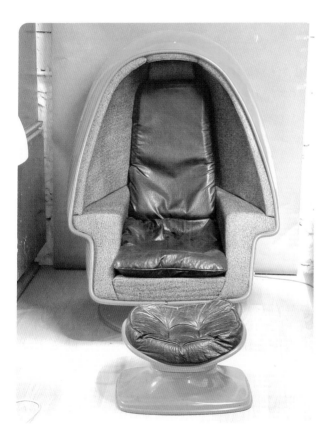

Chests of Drawers

Chests of drawers and their tall cousin, the tallboy, are useful items, and are therefore sought by collectors.

As they are virtually essential items in the home, chests of drawers have always been made in large quantities, and pieces in pine, made for the modest-income household, are not difficult to find. More rare, and therefore more valuable, are chests of drawers made in expensive woods and for leading furniture stores.

Dressing Chest

_c.1910 / 167 x 107 x 53cm / £600_

This dressing chest is designed in the Arts and Crafts style. It has two large and three smaller drawers, all still with their original brass handles, which added to the value of the piece. The mirror swings so that its angle can be adjusted.

Nursery Chest

*c.*1930 / 150 x 115cm / £1,850

Ambrose Heal served an apprenticeship in a Warwick furniture workshop before joining his father's furniture shop in London in 1893. It was largely through his work, which was heavily influenced by the Arts and Crafts Movement, that Heal's became one of the best-known furniture shops in England – which it still is. This oak nursery chest is typical of the Heal's style in the 1930s. It has double- and single-panelled doors, three short drawers and two long drawers.

Desks

For much of the twentieth century, desks made for use in the home did not change all that much in their basic style. Then came the computer.

The greatest change in the desk, both for home and office, as the century progressed was in its weight. Solid wooden pieces of furniture, made to last, gave way to simple work surfaces in lighter-weight woods and other materials, including metal and plastic. The computer, with its need of shelves for printer, keyboard and mouse, quickly led to such innovations as slide-out shelves.

Limed Oak Desk

Exact date unknown / 77 x 140 x 80cm / £4,500

A partner's desk with a difference: there is a drinks bar concealed behind curved-panel doors at one end of it. The desk is made of limed oak and was sold accompanied by its two Art Deco chairs, which helps account for the price it fetched.

Writing Desk

_c.1900s / 88 x 121cm / £1,250_

This writing desk/dressing table, was intended for an Edwardian lady's bedroom or dressing room, hence it's elegant prettiness. The desk has a mirrored writing surface above three drawers decorated with brass lattice panels and it stands on straight tapered legs.

Swedish Desk

1920–1930 / 76 x 144cm / £2,900

This Swedish-made free-standing desk has drawers beneath the writing surface and two side cupboards. It is made in the style known in Sweden as Gustavian.

Garden Furniture

Television gardening programmes have boosted demand for garden furniture and ornaments.

The fashion for outdoor living, with even the smallest back garden boasting a good-sized barbecue, has also increased interest in all forms of garden furniture, such as tables, benches and seats, and ornamentation. Sundials, pottery and stone urns, stone and marble models of everything from Greek goddesses to cats, dogs, ducks and geese, and small fountains, have all seen a great increase in sales in recent years.

Bronze Sundial

1900 / diameter 34cm / £2,500

It is, of course, possible to buy a sundial at a garden centre for £100 or so, depending on the stand you choose for it. But it will not have the patina that many years out in all weathers gives to an old sundial. This bronze circular sundial plate dates from the end of Victoria's reign. It bears the arms of the county of Cornwall and is engraved "Sol est Lux et Gloria Mundi, Newton Camborne, 1900."

Garden Bench

Exact date unknown / width 130cm / £395

This pretty garden seat is made of iron. It has a lattice seat with scrolled ironwork back and arms and is supported by shaped legs on pad feet.

French Chair

***c.*1950 / height 87cm /
£680 the set**

This garden chair, one of a set of four, was made in France. It is made of wrought iron and has a pierced geometric design on the seat and the back splat. The back frame and legs are formed of curved and scrolled ironwork.

Mirrors

Ornamental mirrors, especially overmantel mirrors, and looking glasses have seen steadily increasing sales.

Mirrors do not have to be in obviously twentieth-century style to attract attention, and mirrors in recently made but antique-looking frames, in styles ranging from Etruscan to rococo and Victorian, have become increasingly popular with buyers. Wood frames in good condition will help a mirror or looking glass increase in value more quickly than plaster or composition frames.

Mirrored Dressing Table

1920 / 70 x 86 x 45cm / £800

Here is a dressing table with a fairy tale air: made of mirror glass to match Cinderella's glass slipper. The whole top of this Art Deco style table, including the looking glass and the drawer front, is made of mirrors and the drawer has a glass handle. The table is held up on elegant sabred legs.

Walnut Wall Mirror

_c._1920s / 112 x 68cm / £1,250

This large walnut and parcel gilt wall mirror is made in the style of furniture of George II's reign It has a swan neck pediment and beaded edges to both the outer and inner edges of the frame.

Stools

Useful and unobtrusive pieces of furniture, stools inspired some of the century's leading designers.

Stools do not not necessarily have to have a round seat and three or four legs. All sorts of variations are possible, as some of the twentieth century's leading designers proved with their innovative use of new materials and modern styles.

English Oak Stool

1910–1915 / height 82cm / £500 the pair

One of a pair of stools in Art Nouveau style, this stool has an upholstered seat on an oak frame and four tapered square legs. It has a metal ringed stretcher.

French Art Deco Stool

1920–1930 / height 40cm / £1,400 the pair

This is one of a pair of elegant upholstered stools in Art Deco style. The stool stands on scrolled cabriole legs.

Butterfly Stool

_c._1950 / height 46cm / £985

This clever stool, designed by Son Yanagi for Tendo
Mokko, arose out of the experimentation with new
materials and technologies that wartime and post-war
austerity-conscious governments imposed on designers
and manufacturers.

Stool by Verner Panton

_c._1960 / height 43cm / £745

This stool was designed by the Danish
designer Verner Panton five years after
he had established his own studio in
Switzerland. The stool has a wire frame
and retains its original circular suede
padded cover.

Tables

The greatest changes made to the table during the twentieth century were in small, occasional tables.

There is not a great deal that can be changed about the general shape of the dining table, apart from giving it a stand or base rather than legs. With smaller tables, designers could play with materials, shapes and forms, with some interesting results.

Swedish Art Deco Rosewood Table

Exact date unknown / 73 x 150 x 100cm / £3,200

This Swedish-designed table, in the Art Deco style, is made of rosewood, a dark brown hardwood with an attractive stripe or stipple in the grain. It gets its name from its smell when newly cut, not from its flower or colour. Instead of legs, the table has a lyre-shaped support on a splayed base, a style not uncommon in furniture made during the first half of the twentieth century.

Occasional Tables

1950 / 42.5 x 42.5 x 60cm (largest) / £1,400

Sets of small tables, often called nests of tables, are popular pieces of furniture in small rooms because they can be stored away when not in use. These wood occasional tables, made in Germany by Rosenthal, have gilt porcelain plaques inlaid on the tops.

Sofa Table

c.1900 / 47.5 x 72.5cm / £1,250

This sofa table is made in the style of the Arts and Crafts designer, C. F. A. Voysey. The plank top is supported on tapered legs. The table has an underiler, with stylized heart motifs on either side, and with a storage area for papers.

Wine Table

1900–1915 / 47 x 26cm / £169

A wine table, large enough to put a glass of wine down on but small enough to fit unobtrusively beside a chair or sofa, is a useful piece of sitting room furniture. This attractive version has satinwood banding and a central inlaid flower on its circular top. It stands on a turned column with a tripod base.

Walnut & Chrome Table

c.1980 / height 58cm / £365

The Edwardian sitting room's wine table has become an ashtray table – though there is room for a drink, too. This small circular walnut table stands on a teak pedestal and circular base with metal turned legs.

Modernist Table

c.1930 / 51 x 60cm / £185

Firmly in the Modernist style that grew out of Art Deco, this table can be used as a library table or a cocktail cabinet. It is made from oak with rossbanded decoration and is raised on moulded bracket feet.

Art Deco Table

c.1940s / 70 x 53cm / £225

This two-tier circular oak table in Art Deco style has square tapered supports. Its lower shelf makes it a useful occasional table in the sitting room or a telephone table in the hall.

Walnut Side Table

c.1905 / 52 x 40cm / £650

The quality of the design and carving on this table suggests to experts that it may be the work of C. R. Ashbee and the Guild of Handicraft, both well-known in the English Arts and Crafts Movement. The square-topped table with spiral-turned legs and stretchers is made of oak.

Coffee Table

c.1950s / 51 x 100cm / £495

Twentieth-century designers brought the nineteenth century's sofa table out from behind the sofa, lowered its legs and sat it in front of the sofa, where it became as useful for magazines, newspapers and the feet of TV watchers as for coffee. This circular oak coffee table has turned supports and a circular moulded stretcher, andis raised on bun feet.

Glass

The decorative beauty and inherent fragility of glass makes it one of the most satisfying of all antiques to collect. Treated with care, good-quality, well-designed glass increases in value with the passing of time.

The production of high-quality glass of all kinds continued apace in the twentieth century, both building on a tradition going back to classical times and departing from it in many innovative ways. Perfecting the arts of layering, pressing, engraving and staining helped the century's glassmakers produce outstandingly fine work.

Among the greatest of the many glassmaking centres in the world were Murano, in the Venetian lagoon, where glass had been made for centuries, the Orrefors company in Sweden, Iittala in Finland and Corning in the United States. Corning were responsible, early in the century, for the invention of Pyrex, a heat-resistant, low-expansion oven glassware.

At the beginning of the twentieth century glass design and production was dominated by the Art Nouveau movement and the glass produced by designers working in the style, such as Gallé and the Daum brothers in France and Louis Comfort Tiffany in the United States produced work that is still amongst the most-sought-after of all twentieth-century glass.

The free-flowing "new look", based on curves and organic shapes, that affected design from fashion to furniture in the 1950s was ideally suited to being expressed in the highly malleable medium of glass, and glass objects from this period are also very popular among collectors.

While much twentieth-century glass, modestly priced when first sold, has increased considerably in value, the highest prices are still reserved for the highest quality glass. Important pieces should be signed or numbered, or the artist or studio of origin should be clearly defined.

The condition of any piece of glass is of paramount importance in assessing its likely future value. Ideally, there should be no chips or cracks. In particular, with overlaid glass there should be no separation between the different layers of glass. Sometimes valuable vases that have been damaged on the rim are cut down and re-ground, giving the vase a fore-shortened look that may only be judged by an expert inspecting the balance of the design.

Bowls, Vases & Decorative Glass

Decorative glass objects made by the great glassmakers become works of art, not just items for practical use.

As the twentieth century progressed, the great glassmakers designed work that went beyond the simply practical and created conceptual sculpture meant to be admired.

Italian Glass Sculpture

1970 / height 25cm / £4,000

The wonderfully satisfying curves of this piece of glass sculpture help ensure its value as a work of art as much as a fine example of the glassmaker's craft. Made by Italian glass artist Livio Seguso, it contains within the glass red, yellow, green and turquoise freeform shapes.

The Wave

c.1980s / 42 x 39cm / £5,750

This piece of glass sculpture, made by British glassmaker Colin Reid, is very different from the one above. The artist has given this striking work a specific name, "The Wave", and has shaped it in the form of a breaking wave. It is made of clear glass with internal colouring of blues, grey and rust. Its value reflects the intricacy of the work.

Overlay Cameo Vase

c.1900 / height 17cm / £600

Emil Gallé was a leader of the Nancy School of applied arts in France at the end of the nineteenth century. Particularly interested in glass, he developed a way of decorating glass that involved melting pieces of different coloured glass into the basic body of the piece and then carving and acid-etching it to produce overlay decoration. This typical Gallé vase has the overlay cameo work for which he is famous. The pattern on the vase is a design of pink orchids and green leaves and steams.

Daum Enamelled Vase

1900 / height 21 cm / £3,500

The Nancy glassmakers Jean-Louis August Daum and his brother, Jean-Antonin, were inspired by the success of Gallé's glass to change their own rather conservative output in the early 1890s and were soon producing glass, much of it in the Art Nouveau style, that is now very highly-prized among collectors. This splay-lipped vase has a summer scene with enamelled flowers. Nature was one of the main inspirations of artists working in the Art Nouveau style.

Small Gallé Vase

1900 / height 15cm / £1,900

Emile Gallé designed his glass in a wide range of shapes and forms.
He seems to have particularly liked forms with pronounced curves,
and this small vase is a a very satisfying version
of the curved form. In the true spirit of Art
Nouveau, Gallé also turned to nature as
the inspiration for many of his designs. This
vase has a purple foliate design on a
graduated blue and yellow background.

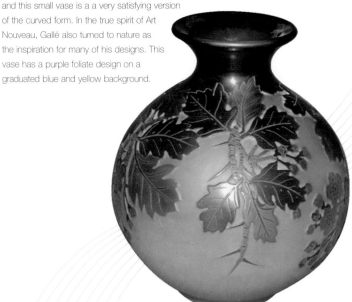

Scandinavian Green Glass Vase

1950 / height 29cm / £180

This conical form glass vase displays the cool style typical of glassware made in Scandinavia in the post-World War II period. The green glass has blue abstract inclusions.

Antonio Da Ros Glass

*c.***1960 / height 29cm / £600**

This clear glass conceptual sculpture was designed by Antonio Da Ros for the Murano glassmaker Cenodese. The piece, which has a dark blue teardrop and secondary droplet within the clear glass, is very much in the sculptural glass style pioneered by the great Venetian glass-maker and designer, Paolo Venini.

Mosaic Vase

1998 / height 29cm / £1,500

This striking vase in baluster form ends twentieth-century glassmaking on a very high note. Designed by "Murrina", the mosaic pattern on the vase is based on a blue and yellow organic design.

Cobweb Vase by Ferro

1998 / height 28cm / £1,500

Another impressive piece of late twentieth-century glass, this yellow vase's bulbous proportions are offset by the raised splayed circular foot on which it stands. The Murano-based glassmaker, V. Ferro, put a black cobweb pattern on the yellow glass. Ferro made glass with a similar mosaic pattern for the Venice Biennale of 1998, emphasizing the fact that this kind of glassware is an art form.

Blue "Cactus" Vase

c.1950 / height 44cm / £1,200

Never was blue glass used so
dramatically as for this extraordinary
piece of glassware. Made by
Recardo Licata for Murano, the
vase's shape and pattern design
was called "Cactus" and was
produced in other colours.

Drinks Glass

Clear, light and strong, glass is an ideal material for making holders for drinks.

Drinking habits and fashions changed greatly during the twentieth century. The 1920s saw the birth of the cocktail, which needed its own kind of drinking glass and its own kind of mixing jug. Social habits changed, too, with eating and drinking out, rather than in the home, becoming the norm rather than an occasional treat. Such changes led to parallel changes in the design, range and variety of glassware made to meet the requirements of the new fashions.

Murano Glasses

c.1960s / height 13.5cm / £200

The exuberant colouring and free-form shape of these glasses is typical of much European design in the 1960s, when the feeling of freedom and lack of restraint expressed in popular music and cinema found their way into many other areas of life. These globular-form glasses on circular bases were produced by the Murano firm of Barovier & Toso.

Italian Glass Decanter

**Exact date unknown /
height 50cm / £550**

The Murano-based glass manufacturer, Cenodese,
designed and produced this red glass decanter. It
has an exceptionally tall glass stopper.

Whitefriars
Martini Jug

*c.*1962 / height 36cm / £95

The long-established English glassworks, Whitefriars,
was based in London in the nineteenth century, when
one of their most popular products was paperweights.
The company produced some very interesting and
unusual glassware in the 1960s and 1970s, much of it
designed by Geoffrey Baxter. This stylish martini jug in
kingfisher blue glass with a clear glass handle was part
of a range called "Whitefriars Studio" by Peter Wheeler.

Scent Bottles

Glass scent bottles have for centuries been among the most stylish items on women's dressing tables.

Twentieth century woman's regard for expensive perfume as an essential fashion accessory created a hugely profitable industry. For perfume sellers, including leading fashion houses whose scents brought them bigger profits than the clothes they designed, it was essential to get their latest scent noticed in a crowded market. The beautiful bottles, often created by leading glassware designers, in which they sold their product became major sales attractions in themselves and are now collectors' items and future antiques.

Turquoise Scent Bottle

c.1910 / height 12cm / £110

This turquoise-coloured opaque glass scent bottle has an elegantly curved handle and stopper. A gold foliage design with ruby glass droplets among the leaves curls over the bulbous body of the bottle. White stems curl up and over the base. The bottle was sold with a pair of small decorative vases carrying a complementary design.

Czechoslovakian Scent Bottle

1920 / height 12cm / £58

Glass made in Czechoslovakia before World War II was renowned for its colour and elegance. This scent bottle, designed and patterned in true Art Deco style, has a large pink silk tassel which complements the smokey glass of the bottle well.

Red Glass Scent Bottle

1920 / height 14cm / £168

Art Deco style meets the Jazz Age in this deep red glass scent bottle. The bottle has an opaque glass stopper in the shape of a feather and a tassel (not seen in the photograph).

Glass Scent Bottle

*c.*1920 / height 14.5cm / £445

A silver stopper has long been the mark of an expensive scent bottle, designed for fashionable ladies' dressing tables. This cut-glass bottle has a particularly generous-sized silver stopper encrusted with flowers and decorated with a foliate design.

Art Deco Bottle

*c.*1920 / height 14.5cm / £135

An incised geometric design, typical of Art Deco, marks this elegant rectangular scent bottle. In contrast to the body of the bottle, the stopper is circular faceted and lozenge-shaped.

Paperweights

The twentieth century saw a strong revival in the production of glass paperweights.

The paperweight-making business in Europe was dominated by French glassmaking houses in the nineteenth century, with such names as Baccarat, Clichy and St Louis producing much very high-quality work. In the twentieth century paperweight-making, which had diminished somewhat, became an important part of glassmakers' output again. In Britain, companies making high-quality paperweights included the long-established firm of Whitefriars of London and the newer paper-weight companies founded in Scotland by Paul Ysart.

Murano Paperweight

*c.*1960 / diameter 23cm / £325

This large and striking paperweight, made by Murano, has a compressed globular form. Filling it is an abstract pattern of blue, white, lime green, pink and gold colours.

Whitefriars Paperweight

1976 / diameter 8cm / £195

The glassmaking firm of Whitefriars of London has included paperweights in its output since the nineteenth century. This 1970s paperweight, in traditional hemispherical shape and design, has six rings of composite cog-wheels of indigo, white, blue, yellow and red, around a central cane.

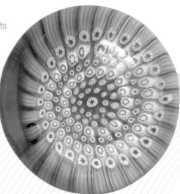

Circular Italian Paperweight

1960 / diameter 7cm / £55

Paperweights have long featured strongly in the output of Italy's glassmakers, and floral themes are not uncommon. This circular paperweight has a silver bubble effect within it and a pattern of stylized pink and white flowers with lime green borders.

Prince Philip Paperweight

1976 / diameter 7.5cm / £179

Baccarat is one of the great glassmaking houses of France, whose paperweights, especially those made in the first half of the nineteenth century, are among the most widely collected. The company stopped producing paperweights from the mid-nineteenth century, starting up again after World War II. This sulphite paperweight, produced by Baccarat, is in facetop form with six lozenge cuts, and is printed with a bust of Prince Philip in uniform.

Baccarat Paperweight of Prince Charles

1976 / diameter 7.5cm / £195

A companion paperweight to the one of Prince Philip above, this sulphite paperweight is in facet form, with six lozenge cuts. The central bust of the Prince of Wales shows him in uniform.

Jewellery

The demand for jewellery is as strong today as ever it was. Current fashion is so relaxed and informal that jewellery from any period is acceptable wear.

The collectors' market for jewellery with antique potential was in a state of constant change throughout the twentieth century, mirroring the rapid changes in fashion that have affected jewellery as much as any other art form. As the work of a decade or particular fashion period and the aesthetic criteria which guided its design and form were re-assessed and even re-cycled, so its jewellery, both inexpensive and valuable, becomes more sought-after. If the jewellery is still in its presentation case, so much the better – it will be all the more valuable, particularly if the name on the case is that of a leading jewellery house.

Art Nouveau and Art Deco jewellery are very popular with today's collectors, the latter being particularly innovative in its design and use of materials. It offered designers a new freedom to experiment with styles, techniques and materials hitherto little used in jewellery-making. This freedom of expression became a prominent feature of twentieth-century jewellery, whether expensive or popular.

Collectors of jewellery should remember that the majority of items found on stalls in antique markets and fairs are second-hand and will have been subjected to some wear and tear. Settings, chain links and fastenings should all be carefully checked before the item is worn.

Burmese Ruby Ring

1930 / £2000

Rubies from the town of Mogok in Upper Burma have for centuries been very highly prized – and very rare. Even when the British were in control of Burma, the number of high-carat rubies mined was small, and there has been very little ruby mining since World War II. All this makes this Art Deco-style ring fitted with four large Burmese rubies valuable indeed. The rubies are surrounded by diamonds and the gems are in a gold setting.

Navajo Ring

c.1970s / £169

Jewellery designed by the Navajo people of the American south-west was very popular, especially among young people for much of the second half of the century. This splendid silver Navajo ring has two oval turquoise stones, probably from Arizona which is a main source for this bluey-green type of turquoise, set within a feather design.

French Brooch

1950 / height 7cm / £85

Interest in jewellery made in the 1950s has greatly increased in recent years, as people have come to appreciate the light-hearted freedom from care that imbued much of the design of the period. This French brooch is styled as a pair of lady's legs, their smoothness and colour suggesting the nylon stockings that were now cheap and readily available after the privations and rationing of World War II in Europe. The red high-heeled shoes and garters studded with paste stones give the brooch a flirtatious air.

Padlock Brooch

1940 / diameter 2cm / £120

This heart-shaped brooch in the shape of a padlock
and key was designed by the American jewellery maker,
Castlecliff. The paste "diamonds" on the padlock and key
are set in sterling silver. Paste is a brilliant and heavy form of
glass, much used in cheap jewellery because it looks
superficially like diamonds.

Art Nouveau Brooch

1900 / length 3cm / £480

The most influential design style of the late nineteenth and early twentieth centuries, Art Nouveau, with its curls and scrolls, was an ideal design style for jewellery. One of the biggest purveyors of the Art Nouveau style in England was Liberty's large shop in Regent Street, London. This 9ct gold brooch set with a turquoise and baroque pearl drop is marked "Liberty & Co."

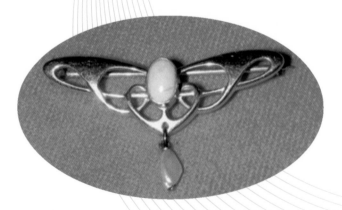

Zuni
Pendant

_c._1940 / diameter 7cm / £950

This ornate pin pendant shows an eagle dancer. An attractive range of semi-precious and other materials, including turquoise, spiney oyster shell, jet and mother-of-pearl are set on a silver base with beading. The style of the piece is very typical of the art of the Zuni people, who are a native American tribe from south-western America, now living in the state of New Mexico.

Pearl & Diamond Necklace

c.1905 / length 6cm / £3,950

Diamonds and pearls were a favourite gem combination for Victorian and Edwardian ladies. This necklace, with its design mixing pearl and diamond droplets and swags, was intended to lie gracefully on the wearer's breast above her low-cut decolletage. It was not necessarily worn alone. Queen Alexandra, for instance, would probably have worn a choker made of several pearl and diamond strands above it.

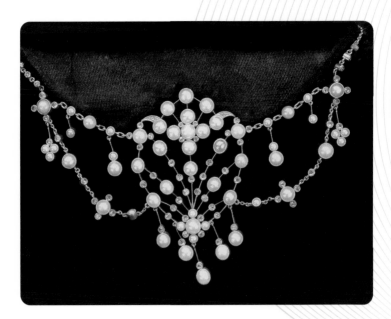

Suffragette Brooch/Pendant

_c._1910 / length 7cm / £1,975

This charming piece of jewellery, which may be worn as either a pendant or a brooch, was designed to be worn by a woman wishing to show her support for the Suffragettes' campaign for votes for women. The gems in the piece – pearls, a large peridot in the centre and pink tourmalines – are the white, green and pink colours of the Suffragette movement.

Music

Communications were revolutionized in the twentieth century. The effect on all forms of music of inventions like the radio, TV and its offshoots the video and DVD players, and mobile tape and CD players, was also revolutionary.

Music, once very much the preserve of the relatively few who had access to musical instruments or were able to listen to it in concert halls or private homes, became available to a very wide audience indeed. Or perhaps it would be more correct to say "two very wide audiences", because the musical world tends to divide into two very broad and often overlapping categories – classical and popular.

It is from the many-stranded world of popular music that most of the twentieth century's musical antiques of the future come. While musical instruments, especially guitars, are high on the music collector's list, other items connected with rock and pop music-making, such as amplifiers and microphones, are also highly collectable. So, too, are vinyl records in good condition and in their original covers or sleeves.

Musical instruments, both old and new, are very collectable. Whether the instrument is a Steinway grand piano or a Gibson guitar, the collector needs to take into account the same basic factors. These are the quality of the materials that been used, the quality of the craftsman- ship that has gone into its making, and the quality of the musical sound that the instrument makes. In many cases, of course, the maker's name on the instrument is a good guide to the likely quality of all three factors.

If the instrument is a rock guitar, then an even better name to have on it, from the collector's point of view, in that of the rock musician who played it. Famous players often sign their instruments for charity.

Popular music led to the creation of the juke-box, the twentieth century's very own version of the long-popular mechanical music maker. There is nothing shy and retiring about a juke-box: unlike musical boxes and wind-up mechanical birds and musical toys, the juke-box needs plenty of space to do it justice. This does not prevent it being a highly collectable and therefore pricey twentieth-century antique.

Mechanical Music

Musical items played by mechanical rather than human action have made good prices in recent years.

The American juke-box, among the century's most popular coin-in-the-slot machines, is also popular with collectors, especially ones that were made in the 1940s, 1950s and 1960s.

Rock-Ola 1448 Juke-box

1955 / 141 x 76cm / £5,000

Juke-boxes have increased enormously in value in the past decade or so, with the highest prices being paid for complete and working units. This American Rock-Ola 1448 juke-box, in chrome and bakelite, was sold with 120 selections. The fact that it was made in the rock 'n' roll era, with which the juke-box was synonymous, adds to its value.

Singing Bird Musical Box

_c._1900s / height 28cm / £1,750

Music boxes in the form of singing birds in a cage were popular items from
before the eighteenth century: William Hogarth included one very like this in
his painting "The Graham Children". This singing bird in a polished brass
cage with a round embossed brass base was probably made by Bontems,
a leading maker of such objects.

Mystic 478 Juke-box

1978–1979 / 136 x 104cm / £1,500

This Mystic 478 juke-box made by Rock-Ola, a prolific American maker of juke-boxes, is made in wood and chrome. It benefits from advances in microchip technology by having a digital micro computer music system and 200 selections.

Dog Model Gramophone

1910 / 70 x 65cm / £1,950

The small dog listening to his master's voice coming out of the gramophone horn became one of the most famous company logos of the recording world, that of HMV. The gramophone photographed here with a model of the dog beside it is an early HMV Junior Monarch, Model No. 3, gramophone in laminated wood. Its original brass horn and concert soundbox are both fully functional.

Carillon Musical Box

c.1900 / 22.5 x 56.25cm / £4,900

The nine individually played bells in this carillon musical box are each surmounted by a dove. The box, made by L'Epée, is made of rosewood and has a marquetry design of pipes, a harp and a lute inlaid on the lid. Eight airs, listed on the inside of the lid, are pinned on a 33cm cylinder.

Musical Instruments

The guitars of rock musicians are among the most sought-after of modern musical instruments.

The international market for musical instruments made in the twentieth century has grown considerably, with particularly keen interest being shown in the instruments played by the great performers and composers of the rock era. Guitars attract the biggest interest, although when Elton John put one of his grand pianos up for sale a couple of years ago, the bidding, from all over the world was frantic. If a musical instrument does not have a great name attached to it, it must be musically excellent if it is to be worth a great deal of money.

Gibson Guitar

1963 / £8,500

This custom-made Gibson guitar in a sunburst finish has block markers and a left-handed ebony fingerboard. Its serial number is ES335. Left-handed guitars are rare and are therefore keenly sought-after, which means they usually fetch a premium price.

Gibson Flying Vee

1958 / £55,000

The great guitar-making company, Gibson, made only 100 of the Flying Vee guitar. It is the Holy Grail of vintage solid body guitars, which helps account for the huge price paid for this example, which has a korina wood body.

Acoustic Guitar

1929 / £26,000

This very fine Martin acoustic guitar, model no. 00045, has Brazilian rosewood back and sides and pearl inlay.

Les Paul Guitar

1954 / £7,000

This Gibson Les Paul guitar has a gold top. It once belonged to Richie Sanbora of the American rock band Bon Jovi.

Fender Stratocaster

1960 / £18,500

Only five versions of this Fender Stratocaster are believed to have been made. This custom-ordered metallic blue sparkle Stratocaster has a slab rosewood fingerboard.

Ebonised Piano

1958 / length 208cm / £39,500

Pianos, both upright and grand models, vary greatly in price, depending on their maker and date of construction. This Model B Steinway & Sons black ebonised piano in a high gloss finish was fully rebuilt by its makers before it was sold.

Rosewood Satin Piano

1906 / height 135cm / £21,500

This handsome upright piano was made in Hamburg at the beginning of the century. A Model K. piano, it has a rosewood satin case with inlay veneer and was fully rebuilt by Steinway & Sons, one of the best and longest-established names in the piano-making business.

Rock & Pop

The memorabilia and ephemera created by the rock and pop music industry offers collectors many treasures.

Vinyl records and their covers are increasing in value now that so few of them are being produced and make worthwhile investments. LPs from the great days of rock and pop music command high prices if they are in good condition and still have their covers; if they are the work of one of the really big names then prices can be very high. Apart from records, there is a great deal of memorabilia and paper ephemera of the rock music world ready to be found by collectors, much of it produced as part of big-budget advertising and marketing campaigns.

"Instant Karma", Lennon

1971 / £117

John and Yoko Lennon's "Instant Karma" long-playing vinyl disc was produced by the notorious American record producer Phil Spector. The apple on the label harks back to the days of The Beatles.

The Police Singles Box

1990 / 18 x 18cm / £195

The perfect gift for a rock fan, this embossed wooden box contains 10 gold vinyl singles together with a picture disc by The Police.

Rolling Stones Album

1971 / 30 x 30cm / £700

An album cover from the great days of cover design packages an export edition of the Rolling Stones' great album, *Stone Age*.

Tote Bag with Duran Duran Singles

1985 / 30 x 35cm / £75

A clever marketing gimmick for the 1980s pop group, Duran-Duran, this tote bag contains five 12-inch ("maxi") singles recorded by the band.

Manic Street Preachers Single

1988 / 18 x 18cm / £995

A considerable amount was added to the sales value of this Double A-side single, "Suicide Alley Tennessee", from Manic Street Preachers, because of the presence in the sleeve of a letter from the band, written on lined green notepaper.

Bob Dylan Record

1961 / £735

A very youthful Bob Dylan gazes out from the cover of his first recording, called simply *Bob Dylan*, which was produced by leading record producer John Hammond and manufactured and distributed by CBS.

Elvis

1971 / £1,800

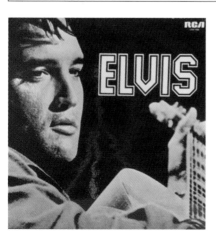

RCA, the manufacturer and distributor of this record by Elvis Presley, saw no need to put the recording's name, which was "You'll Never Walk Alone," on the front of the cover. *Elvis* was all that was needed to guarantee big sales.

Photography

The invention of photography in the nineteenth century gave the world a new art form that transformed the way in which people recorded life in the twentieth century.

Both the camera and the photographs it takes have become valuable collectors items. When the Eastman Kodak company of America introduced its box camera, with its ready-loaded roll film and a widely available developing and printing service in 1888, it gave everyone, young and old, the chance to record everything about the life around them. It also meant that today's collectors must decide from the outset what it is they want to collect if they are not to be overwhelmed by the sheer quantity of what is available.

There is an extra bonus to be gained from collecting cameras: choose well, and the camera will be usable for years to come. Dealers in old cameras recommend SLR cameras as good future investments, mainly because of the onset of the digital age.

As for photographs, an area with good investment potential is that of the celebrity photograph. Photos of famous people, from politicians to film stars, including those who have fallen out of the public eye, are often good investments. If it is known that only a few prints of a photograph were put into circulation, they are probably also good investments because rarity usually leads to an increase in value.

Cameras

Cameras for amateurs have been around since 1888, so the choice available to the collector is vast.

Anyone purchasing an older camera should ensure that it is in good working order and that the lens is not scratched or damaged. The condition of the body and the shutter mechanism is also an important consideration when assessing a camera's value. The film used in it should also be checked, as some older types of film are no longer made. As with other collectables, a complete camera set in its original box should prove to be a good investment.

Rolleiflex TLR Camera

> **1960s / 15 x 10cm / £649**

The Rolleiflex twin lens reflex camera was the camera of choice for many professional photographers in the1960s. It was highly valued because of its very fine quality lens and the medium-format film it used, which facilitated high-quality results. This Rolleiflex 2.8F twin lens camera uses standard 120 roll film.

Thornton Pickard Camera

c.1909 / 21 x 25.5cm / £300

This triple extension Thornton Pickard camera uses half-plate sized glass plates, not film. The case is wood and the bellows leather. It is a rising front camera, which means that it is capable of photographing tall buildings without making them look as if they are tapering away at the top.

Midget Coronet Camera

*c.*1930s / 2 x 6cm / £325

The camera as fashion accessory. This Midget Coronet camera,
designed in Art Deco style, has a blue Bakelite case and is fitted with
a Taylor Hobson F10 lens. The colour is very rare.

Mick A Matic

1971 / height 20cm / £49

The perfect first camera for a child, this Mick A Matic camera in the shape of Mickey Mouse is great fun and easy to use. It was made by the American company, Child Guidance Product Inc.

Photographs

A good photograph can rank alongside a work of art as an image of its time. Its potential value is considerable.

The collector of photographs has such a huge choice that it is a good idea to specialise, or at least to be aware of the kind of photograph that will increase in value. Look out for prints that capture a freak or unusual moment, are the work of well-known or up-and-coming photographers, or are from a limited edition printing.

Jackie K

c.1959 / 50.8cm x pro / £2,400

Jacqueline Kennedy Onassis (1929–1994) was the wife of Senator Jack Kennedy when this colour photograph of her was taken by Lambda at an "April in Paris" ball. Her husband became President of the United States in 1960. The photograph is a limited edition, being one of only four signed by the photographer.

Lartigue Silver Gelatin Print

1929 / 30.5 x 35.5 / £4,600

Jacques-Henri Lartigue was one of the leading French photographers of the early twentieth century. His work captured the spirit of the age in a way that few could match. This silver gelatin print, "Solange David, Paris, 1929", is signed on the recto (the front) by the photographer.

Signed Willoughby Print

1962 / 30.5 x 35.5cm / £400

American photographer Bob Willoughby caught the wonderful jazz singer Billie Holliday in full flow in this photograph, "Billie Holliday, Tiffany Club, 1962". This is a silver gelatin print, signed on the verso (the back) by the photographer.

Fair Fun

1938 / length 50.8cm / £225

A famous photograph from a famous magazine, this picture of young women
enjoying themselves on a roller coaster at Southend Fair in England was taken
by Kurt Hutton and published in Picture Post. This version is a modern black
and white, fibre silver gelatin archival photograph, printed in the darkrooms of
the Hulton Getty Picture Collection in a limited edition of 300.

Printed Matter

Printing on paper expanded in many directions during the twentieth century to meet the demands of manufacturers, advertisers and many others. New types were designed and new printing processes, especially for colour, were invented.

So great was the amount of printed matter produced in the twentieth century, much of it connected with everyday items, that this chapter can give only an indication of what may be available to the collector. It concentrates on five key areas in which it is possible to specialise, choosing subjects of particular interest and ignoring the great mass of related material available.

Books were produced throughout the century in unprecedented numbers, despite competition from radio, television and the cinema. In fact, book publishing became very profitable offshoots of all these. For the serious collector, however, the book itself is what matters, and the quality of the binding is often of greater interest than the contents of the book. The binding ceases to have such importance when a book's author is famous and has signed the book. J. K. Rowling's signature on one of her Harry Potter books can be enough to make the book worth several thousand pounds.

Comics and related ephemera such as children's annuals, film fan magazines, rock music magazines and similar publications do not usually command such high prices, but are still worth collecting. In contrast, posters, especially those for important or popular films, can command very high prices indeed, provided they are in good condition and will look good framed and hanging on the wall.

Scripophily is another form of printed paper, popular with collectors, that can look good when framed. Interesting historical connections add to the value of scrip and paper money.

With printed matter, as with all forms of collecting, the buyer needs to be able to distinguish between the fad of today and the object that will have antique value in the future.

Books

Books were published in huge numbers in the twentieth century, spurred on by design and printing innovations.

The collectors' market for books is so large, that would-be investors need to know how to evaluate a book before buying. First editions can fetch very high prices, as can books from collectable authors and illustrators, especially if signed by them. Original dust jackets add to the value of a book, as do slipcases and fine bindings.

Master and Commander

1969 / 15 x 22.5cm / £650

This first edition of Patrick O'Brian's Napoleonic naval warfare novel is in very good condition and has its original dust jacket. Published in by J. B. Lippincott Co., New York and Philadelphia, it preceded the later, English edition published in 1970 by Collins.

Stiff Upper Lip, Jeeves

1963 / 14 x 21cm / £100

This first edition of a later novel in P. G. Wodehouse's series of novels about Bertie Wooster and his "man" Jeeves, is of very good quality. The fact that it has its original dust jacket adds to its value. It was published in New York by Simon and Schuster and preceded the London edition by five months.

Ulysses

1922 / height 26cm / £23,500

James Joyce's *Ulysses* is one of the defining novels of English literature in the twentieth century. This first edition of the novel was limited to 1000 copies on Dutch handmade paper. This boxed copy is one of 750 of the edition that were printed on handmade paper and numbered, the number on this one being 501 (from a number sequence of 251–1000). The edition was published by Shakespeare and Company, 12 Rue de l'Odeon, Paris.

Harry Potter Set

1997–2000 / 20 x 13cm / £27,500

J. K. Rowling's stories about Harry Potter and his friends – and enemies – at Hogwarts School of Witchcraft and Wizardry took the world of children's books by storm when they were first published. While individual first editions in good condition have been fetching high prices, especially if signed by the author, a set of first editions, all signed, is very rare indeed. This set, comprising *The Philosopher's Stone*, *The Chamber of Secrets*, *The Prisoner of Azkaban* and *The Goblet of Fire*, were all published by Bloomsbury, London.

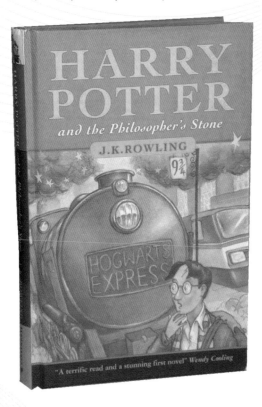

Mobile Etude

1962 / 23.6 x 18.7cm / £5,000

The full title of this magnificently designed book, dedicated to the American artist
Jackson Pollock and produced in France is *Mobile Etude pour une Representation
des Etats Unis*. It is one of 25 numbered copies with contemporary black leather-
backed grey boards and an intricate mosaic onlay of coloured paper cubes. The
book is preserved in its original grey board cover with perspex back and matching
grey board slipcase. It was published by Gallimard in Paris.

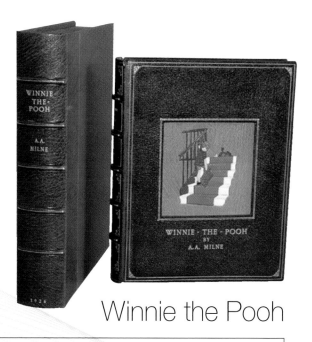

Winnie the Pooh

1926 / 23 x 17cm / £8,500

The Winnie the Pooh stories by A. A. Milne, with illustrations by Ernest H. Shephard, are among the most treasured of twentieth-century children's books. This edition of *Winnie the Pooh*, limited to 1,350 copies, has a wonderful onlaid binding, with decorations by E. H. Shephard. Copies were numbered and signed by Milne and Shephard. The edition was published by Methuen andCo., London.

Comics

Strip-cartoon comics appeal to everyone, children and adults alike, and so are published in large numbers.

The comic, its pages filled with stories in strip cartoon form, is among the most popular of those paper items that collectors gather together under the name "ephemera". Comics acquire value because, although published in large print runs, they are also thrown away in large numbers. Apart from ephemera fairs, good places to look for comics are car boot sales, charity shops and school fairs, all places where the detritus cleared from attics and the bedrooms of grown-up children tend to end up in large piles.

Girl

1951 / £25

The modern 1950s British girl, guided by mothers and aunts who had done much that men could do during World War II, expected that publishing aimed at them would talk about more than how to get on at school. This first edition of a comic for girls printed with colour throughout, has a carefully thought-out attraction – the adventures of an all-girl flying crew – on its cover. *Girl* was published by Hulton Press.

Viz Comic

1981 / £4

This is issue number 7 of *Viz*, one of the first adult humour "alternative" comics. Judged by present-day standards, its jokes seem aimed at giggling schoolboys.

The Lone Ranger

1958 / £6

The Lone Ranger was a familiar figure in American comics, riding the range of the West fighting bad men and righting wrongs. This comic book, published by Gold Key, dates from quite late in his career.

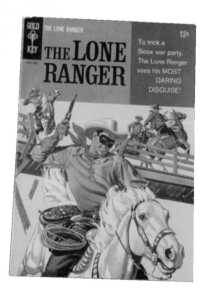

Spider-Man

1963 / £140

Added value has been given to old Spider-Man comics by the recent successful film about the exploits of the building-climbing righter of wrongs. The Amazing Spider-Man story "The Enforcers" No. 10 was published by Marvel Comics.

Superman

1943 / £230

Superman was the twentieth-century's greatest and most dashing comic hero. As it says on the front of Superman No. 20, he was "the world's greatest adventure-strip character". This edition of his comic adventures was published a year or so after America joined in World War II, so naturally Superman is coming to the rescue of men whose ship has been torpedoed.

Ephemera

Fan magazines and annuals featuring characters from popular comics are highly collectable ephemera.

The more popular the characters featured in such magazines and annuals, the more likely they are to realise good prices.

ZigZag

1976 / £4

ZigZag was a British-produced monthly magazine about the rock music performers and composers of the period. Issue number 65 devoted its main feature article to the Beach Boys.

Amazing Stories

1954 / £5

Volume I, Issue no. 5 of the sci-fi magazine *Amazing Stories* included a story by the now famous science-fiction writer Phillip K. Dick. His novel, *Do Androids Dream of Electric Sheep?*, provided the basic premise for the sci-fi movie *Blade Runner*.

The Beano Book, 1973

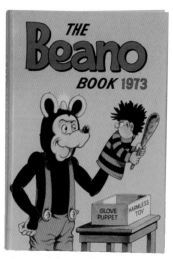

1973 / £20

Scottish publishers, D. C. Thompson, like other comic publishers in Britain, began bringing out annuals devoted to their best-selling comics and the characters in them in the 1950s. The hard-covered annuals were usually published in time to make stocking fillers at Christmas. The cover of this annual features the *Beano*'s leading character, Dennis the Menace.

Batman Annual

1964 / £20

The Batman Annual for 1964–5, while including stories about "the celebrated crime-fighting duo, Batman & Robin," also made space for other comic characters, such as John Jones from Mars and Congo Bill.

Film Posters

Movie posters are printed in great numbers and distributed with the film's marketing material. Unless the film or its stars are very famous, prices are reasonable.

Posters make good starting points for collectors of ephemera. They are fun to have, usually very lively in their design, and, with certain exceptions, reasonably priced. Collectors should aim to put at the top of their "must have" list posters of great films and their actors and actresses. Because there are so many of them, it is a good idea to narrow the initial search by looking for personal favourites, whether films or their stars.

Film posters, especially of well-known American films or with celebrated stars, that were printed and distributed in small countries have become rare and are therefore usually good investments.

The condition and rarity of a poster enhances its value. Posters that have been properly backed with linen or heavy paper and have been stored flat or rolled, rather than folded, are likely to be good investments.

Moulin Rouge

1952 / 84 x 58cm / £1,800

This poster was designed by Polish artist
Lucjan Jagodzinski to advertise in Poland the
American film *Moulin Rouge*, directed by John
Huston and starring Jose Ferrer as the French
painter Toulouse-Lautrec. The poster is paper-
backed and unfolded, which adds to its value.

Il Diritto
di Uccidere

**1950 / 140 x 99cm /
£3,500**

This original, linen-backed Italian poster for
the Humphrey Bogart film, *In A Lonely Place*,
features the artwork of Anselmo Ballester.

Vertigo

1958 / 83 x 60.5cm / £2,500

Most of the films of director Alfred Hitchcock have been internationally
successful, and their posters are all very collectable. This poster was
designed for the internationally distributed version of *Vertigo*, and
features the director's face in the design.

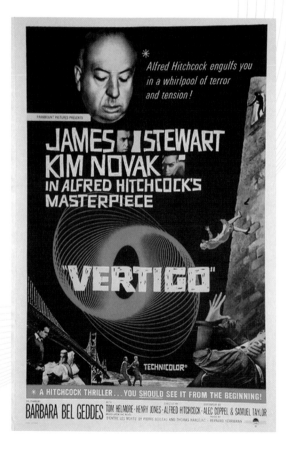

Yellow Submarine

1969 / height 104cm / £12,500

The American-designed poster for the Beatles' film, *Yellow Submarine*, uses 1960s psychedelic art to great effect. There is also a hint of Peter Blake's great album cover design for "Sgt. Pepper's Lonely Hearts Club Band" in this one-sheet poster.

Scripophily & Paper Money

Wealth in paper form, which can include paper money, bonds, stock and share certificates, treasury notes and bank cheques holds a particular fascination.

In the financial and business world, the word "scrip" can mean several things, including a receipt or certificate, shares or stock issued to shareholders in a scrip issue, or a certificate that part of the issue price of a debenture or share has been paid. For antique collectors, scripophily covers a wider area of financial dealings, encompassing other paper forms such as bank cheques and treasury notes.

To have any significant value, a bond, share certificate, note or other form of paper money must be printed on paper that is not torn, stained or badly creased. Printing errors, rarity of production and condition are all factors that play a part in dictating the value of a piece. However, a buyer should never forget that printing errors and condition can indicate, not rarity, but a forgery.

Many larger notes, share certificates and bonds look good framed and hanging as interesting and decorative additions to a hallway or study.

Railway Bond

1911 / £18

This handsomely printed bond was issued by the
Brazil Railway Company. It includes a romantic picture
of a steam train crossing a viaduct in country that
looks more European than South American.

Scottish Banknote

1915 / £85

This Scottish bank note, for £1, was issued during World War I by the National Bank
of Scotland. It is ornately designed, probably in a bid to make forgery difficult.

Although the parliaments
of England and Scotland
were united by the Act of
Union in 1707, Scotland
retained the power to
issue its own banknotes.

Silver, Pewter & Metalware

Twentieth-century silversmiths well upheld the centuries-old tradition of making objects of great beauty in silver and other metals. Very fine pieces were made in the century's great styles, from Art Nouveau to Modern.

Collectors of twentieth-century silver find much to excite them in silver designed in the Art Nouveau style, the curved lines of which suited being incorporated into silver and pewter objects. Vases, bowls, mirrors and photograph frames are some of the smaller objects in Art Nouveau style which may still be found by enthusiasts. Among the less ornately styled silver and silver plate from the mid-twentieth century onwards, cruet sets, cutlery, coasters and tea services are popular.

The great advantage of collecting silver and pewter is that they are hall-marked. This not only guarantees their quality but also provides information about the maker, date and place of manufacture.

Silver plate, which is not solid silver, nevertheless has a colour and quality that is very attractive. It was invented in the eighteenth century by

Thomas Bolsover, whose discovery that melted silver would adhere to copper led to Sheffield plate. Makers of silver plate became known as cutlers, as they still are in Sheffield today.

Good quality pewter relies on its fine lines and proportions, and its shape should define its purpose. Any embellishments on pewter objects, such as mouldings on rims or bases, should be as simple as possible, in keeping with the colour and smooth quality of the metal. Because it is soft and malleable, pewter is quite easily dented and otherwise damaged. Poor repairwork on such damage lowers the value of a piece.

Towards the end of the twentieth century, other metals such as bronze, chrome and stainless steel, which had tended to get lost sight of amidst designers' enthusiasm for man-made materials like Bakelite and plastics, began to be used again. Good quality items in these metals should increase in value.

Silver

The ready availability of twentieth-century silver does not diminish its value.

Small silver objects that can be used in the home, such as bowls, cream jugs, salt cellars and tea pots, are sensible choices to begin a silver collection with, as utility always adds value to an item.

Gilded Fruit Bowl

1910 / 12 x 24cm / £650

This silver-plated fruit bowl has a gilded interior and a glass liner. It stands on a pedestal foot with a pierced geometric design and the rim has a gadrooned border. The bowl is engraved with the initials "W. M. F.".

Dish Ring

1913 / 10 x 19cm / £3,500

This highly decorated Irish silver dish ring was made in Dublin. Its borders are gadrooned, that is, they are decorated with a series of grooves, ending in a curved lip, with ridges between the grooves. The pierced floral designs are centred with oval cartouches.

Four Lanterns

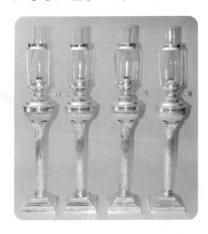

**_c._1900 / height
47cm / £2,500**

These four electro-plated lanterns in
the shape of candlesticks and set on
square plain bases, have their original
glass funnels, which adds to the value
of the set.

Sugar Basket

**1913 / height 14cm /
£675**

This fine silver sugar basket was made by
Charles Stuart Harris of London. It has a
frosted glass liner to hold the sugar.

Champagne Cup

1902 / height 14cm / £1,160

This elegant silver champagne cup with a saucer-shaped bowl was made by William Adams Ltd, a Birmingham silversmith.

Sheffield Caster

1911 / height 13cm / £600

The city of Sheffield was as renowned for its silver and Sheffield plate cutlery and tableware as much as it was for its steel. Although the steel-making has gone, Sheffield still makes cutlery and tableware. This fine silver conical-form caster with a fluted design has a finial top and serpentine base.

Tulip Vase

c.1900 / height 21cm / £680

This tulip-shaped vase with foliate-style handles, is in the Art Nouveau style. It was part of the Tudric range of high-quality, Celtic-inspired pewter and silver ware designed for mass production and sold through Liberty & Co, the London department store.

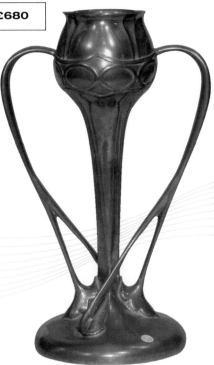

Silver Bowl

1930 / height 16cm / £1,100

A bravura piece, demonstrating the design potential of silver, this bowl with berry fruit decoration is made in a style of silver called "Crumpled Paper".

Wine Labels

1910 / length 5cm / £45

Labels identifying the contents of drinks decanters and jugs have
traditionally been made from silver. These silver labels on chains are
for port, madeira and shrub, a cordial made from different fruits,
spirits and sugar that was popular in Victorian and Edwardian times.

Cocktail Shaker

1920 / height 20cm / £68

The cocktail shaker, an essential item in the Jazz Age's
cocktail cabinet, has seen something of a revival in
use in recent years. This elegantly plain-styled silver-
plate cocktail shaker would look at home on the
modern drinks' tray.

Pewter

The softness and malleability of pewter, which is an alloy of tin, lead and, often, various other metals, has made it a popular metal for household ware for centuries.

The Arts and Crafts Movement and the curved shapes of Art Nouveau design helped make pewter a fashionable metal at the turn of the twentieth century. It was the main metal used by Archibald Knox and others for the Tudric metalware sold by Liberty & Co. Pewter's softness means that it is relatively easily damaged, and repairwork on it should be closely examined before buying. Pewter pieces often display irregular black patches and stains, caused by oxidation; these are easily removed by soaking the item in paraffin.

Pewter Vase

1903 / height 18cm / £950

The Art Nouveau influence is clear in this pewter vase with a green glass liner. It was designed by the leading metalwork designer of the period, Archibald Knox, for Liberty & Co.

Pewter Fruit Bowl

1905 / 11 x 16.5cm / £380

This fruit bowl, comprising a green glass liner in pewter mounts, is designed in the true Art Nouveau style, incorporating organic patterns. It was made by Orivit, a German company that produced many items of pewter-mounted glass.

Tudric Jug

*c.*1900 / height 19cm / £680

This pewter jug is from the Tudric
range of Celtic art-inspired pewter
ware made for Liberty & Co at the turn
of the century. The pattern on it is called
"fish and the sea" and the handle is
brass. It is inscribed "U. C. C.".

Biscuit Barrel

1902 / 15 x 13cm / £1,500

Archibald Knox, a leading designer of his day, much of whose work
was sold by Liberty & Co, designed this pewter biscuit barrel for the
Tudric range. It has blue and green enamelling on the sides.

Metalware

Many different kinds of metalware are used in a wide range of decorative items and household wares.

B ronze, brass, copper and chrome are among the metals used most often in the creation of objects to decorate and for use in the home. Bronze figures, very popular early in the century, are now particularly sought-after by collectors.

Bronze Figure

1921 / height 24cm / £1,100

This bronze figure, entitled "Wind", was exhibited at the Royal Academy in London. It is signed and dated 1921.

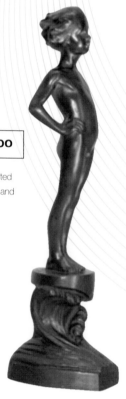

Art Deco Figure

**_c._1925 / height 30cm /
£1,275**

This finely modelled Art Deco-style bronze,
depicting a bare-footed young man holding
a lariat, stands on a marble plinth.

Letter Rack

c.1950 / height 45cm / £45

Coloured wire was a popular material for household items in the 1950s. This letter rack in cat form is made of black wire, formed into a spring for the cat's body. The cat's plastic eyes have rotating eye balls, which perhaps accounts for its rather malevolent expression.

Chrome Coffee Pot

c.1950 / height 24cm / £50

This Italian-designed round coffee pot on three feet has a chrome body and a cork stopper in the spout. It was designed as a companion to a round chrome teapot, also with a cork stopper and standing on three feet.

Bronze Vase

c.1900 / height 27cm / £6,500

A cat's heads look down on field mice, wheat and poppies from beneath the rim of this two-colour patinated gilt bronze vase. It is signed by Leopold Savine, of L. Colin et Cie. It has the Paris founder's mark on it.

Toys, Games & Dolls

Before World War II, the largest producers of toys were based in Germany, where special export versions of toys were also made for selling round the world.

The international market for antique toys is extremely strong. Toy cars are very popular and include those manufactured by the early French C.I.J. Company in the late 1920s, along with British Dinky and Matchbox cars, and the German Orober vans, which have also risen steadily in value. German tinplate toys by Carette, Gunthermann and Lehmann, made between 1900 and 1930, are fetching premium prices. These companies also produced ships, aeroplanes and figures, all of which were remarkable pieces of engineering.

British manufacturers such as Wells, Brimtoy and Chad Valley began to compete with the Continental market in the 1930s and 1940s, making cars, aeroplanes and trains on a cheaper basis. At this time Tri-Ang began to produce small tinplate commercial vehicles with clock-work mechanisms known as Mimic Toys, which are now highly collectable.

Dolls and teddy bears remain hugely popular among toy collectors. The string-jointed teddy bear, first made by Richard Steiff in 1902, has soarer in value over recent decades, with six-figure sums being paid for teddy bears "with a history". Toys worth investing in for the future are those associated with popular books or films, such as the Harry Potter and Lord of the Rings series.

Circus Elephant

1950 / height 14cm / £88

This clockwork circus elephant is still in good working order. It is coloured grey, with blue eyes and long black lashes. Its trappings are brightly coloured in red, white, blue and yellow.

Dalek

1950s / height 12cm / £225

Daleks were the best-known villains in the long-running BBC children's programme, *Dr Who* and many versions of them were produced. This unusual Dalek is made of blue and silver metal.

Clown on Stilts

_c_.1950s / height 20cm / £100

This clever clockwork clown not only walks on stilts, he also plays
the violin. He is dressed in red and white striped trousers, a green
checked top with a red frilled collar and a green hat. He still has
his wind-up key and the brightly printed box in which he was sold.

Set of Metal Soldiers

1950 / height 4cm (each soldier) / £1,500

Britains' scale model soldiers are renowned for their accuracy of detail and excellent modelling. This set of lead, hand-painted soldiers includes mounted soldiers, in the uniforms of Britain's main cavalry regiments, kilted men from Highland regiments, bandsmen and other foot soldiers – enough to mount a battle on the nursery floor or on a scale model battlefield set up on a table top.

Mickey Mouse

_c._1930 / height 33cm / £110

Mickey Mouse was the first, and the most famous, of the many cartoon characters created by Walt Disney. He appeared, looking much like this stuffed toy, in _Steamboat Willie_ (1928), the first cartoon to feature synchronized sound. This velvet padded Mickey Mouse features the wide smiling expression of the cartoon character. It was an early item in what became a virtual Mickey Mouse industry, producing large numbers of toys and games and a Mickey Mouse wristwatch that is now a collector's item.

Snow White

c.1930 / height 44cm / £368

The story of Snow White and the seven dwarfs who looked after her when she was cast out by her wicked stepmother, is one of the great European fairy tales. This french-made Snow White doll has a padded body and composition face and hands. Walt Disney' chose the story for his first feature-length animated cartoon film, *Snow White and the Seven Dwarfs* (1938).

Ferrari Pedal Car

1970 / length 117cm / £250

A scale model on a grand scale, this stylish pedal car would give a small child a
great opportunity to imagine what Grand Prix driving was all about. This red Ferrari
racing car has large rubber tyres and a racing number on the sides and bonnet.

Terrafish

1960 / length 23cm / £275

The moving parts and the yellow spots and large green eyes of this green
Terrafish would have thrilled any child fan of the 1960s Gerry Anderson
children's TV series. It was made by Lakeside Toys of Japan.

Chad Valley Teddy

1950 / height 44cm / £250

This padded teddy bear, with his bright brown glass eyes and pleasant expression, must have delighted the child it was given to.. The teddy was made by Chad Valley, a leading British maker of children's toys.

Baby Doll

_c._1900 / height 26cm / £298

This baby doll, made of porcelain and
with jointed arms and legs, is in the best
tradition of German doll-making at the turn
of the century. The doll has blue eyes,
weighted so that they will close when it
is laid down, carefully painted eyebrows
and bright red cheeks. The doll wears
a matching sleep suit and hat.

Konig & Wernig Doll

_c._1900 / height 24cm / £525

Dolls in this style were made well into the twentieth century.
This one, from the German doll-maker, Konig and Wernig, has
a curly blonde wig, brown glass eyes and a jointed porcelain body. She wears a pretty lilac dress
with small red spots and a pink velvet hat with lace and satin bows.

Conversion Charts

This chart provides a scale of measurements converted from centimetres and metres to feet and inches.

MEASUREMENT CONVERSION CHART

1cm	2/5in	20cm	7 3/4in	1.25m	4ft 1 1/5in
2cm	4/5in	25cm	9 4/5in	1.5m	4ft 11in
3cm	1 1/10in	30cm	11 4/5in	1.75m	5ft 8 9/10in
4cm	1 3/5in	40cm	1ft 3 3/4in	2m	6ft 6 3/4in
5cm	2in	50cm	1ft 7 2/3in	2.25m	7ft 4 3/5in
10cm	3 7/8in	75cm	2ft 5 1/2in	2.5m	8ft 2 2/5in
15cm	5 9/10in	1 m	3ft 3 1/3in	3m	9ft 10 1/10in

This chart provides a scale of prices converted from pounds sterling to Australian dollars, based on a conversion rate of $2.55 to the pound.

AUSTRALIAN CURRENCY CONVERSION CHART

£1	$2.55	£150	$382.50	£2,000	$5,100.00
£5	$12.75	£175	$446.25	£5,000	$12,750.00
£10	$25.50	£200	$510.00	£7,500	$19,125.00
£20	$51.00	£250	$637.50	£10,000	$25,500.00
£25	$63.75	£300	$765.00	£20,000	$51,000.00
£50	$127.50	£400	$1,020.00	£30,000	$76,500.00
£75	$191.25	£500	$1,275.00	£40,000	$102,000.00
£100	$255.00	£750	$1,912.50	£50,000	$127,500.00
£125	$318.75	£1,000	$2,550.00	£100,000	$255,000.00

This chart provides a scale of prices converted from pounds sterling to US dollars, based on a conversion rate of $1.60 to the pound.

US CURRENCY CONVERSION CHART

£1	$1.60	£150	$240.00	£2,000	$3,200.00
£5	$8.00	£175	$280.00	£5,000	$8,000.00
£10	$16.00	£200	$320.00	£7,500	$12,000.00
£20	$32.00	£250	$400.00	£10,000	$16,000.00
£25	$40.00	£300	$480.00	£20,000	$32,000.00
£50	$80.00	£400	$640.00	£30,000	$48,000.00
£75	$120.00	£500	$800.00	£40,000	$64,000.00
£100	$160.00	£750	$1,200.00	£50,000	$80,000.00
£125	$200.00	£1,000	$1,600.00	£100,000	$160,000.00

Index